This can be beautiful
This can be beautiful
This Can Be Beauti
Beautiful THIS CAN
This Can Be Beautif
THIS CAN BE BEAUTIFUL
aut
Be Beautiful TH
This can be b
THIS CAN BE Beautiful
This can be b
an be beautiful
This Can Be

SIMPLE DIY
PROJECTS TO STYLE YOUR
HOME AND REDESIGN YOUR LIFE

TIFFANY PRATT

PHOTOGRAPHY BY TARA McMULLEN

appetite
by RANDOM HOUSE

Appetite by Random House® and colophon are registered trademarks of Penguin Random House LLC.

Library and Archives of Canada Cataloguing in Publication is available upon request.

ISBN: 9780449016930
eBook ISBN: 9780449016947

Photography copyright © Tara McMullen
Book design by Kelly Hill

Printed and bound in China

Published in Canada by Appetite by Random House®,
a division of Penguin Random House Canada Limited

www.penguinrandomhouse.ca

10 9 8 7 6 5 4 3 2 1

appetite
by RANDOM HOUSE | Penguin
Random
House

THIS
BOOK

IS FOR
YOU

CONTENTS

CHAPTER 3
FASHION PLATE
PAGE 46

INTRODUCTION PAGE 1
HOW THIS BOOK WORKS PAGE 4
TIPS & TOOLS PAGE 6

CHAPTER 1
EVERY DAY IS EVER
DAZZLING
PAGE 10

CHAPTER 4
BEAUTY ON DUTY
PAGE 64

CHAPTER 2
HOME IS WHERE THE GLITTER IS
PAGE 28

CHAPTER 7
TIFFANY TRAVELS
PAGE 120

CHAPTER 5
LOVE GESTURES
PAGE 82

CHAPTER 8
HANGIN' WITH THE KIDS
PAGE 140

FINAL THOUGHTS
PAGE 158
ACKNOWLEDGMENTS
PAGE 161
INDEX
PAGE 164

CHAPTER 6
ARTY PARTY
PAGE 100

What you are holding in your soon-to-be-glittered hands is an inspirational, explosive joyride. *This Can Be Beautiful* is not simply the title of this book. It is a choice about the way you think and the way you look at what you already have. When you think "this can be beautiful" about everything you see and touch, beautiful results will follow. If you build your own whimsical dream with your own two hands, your life will come running behind it, wanting to be a part of it all.

Trust me, I know. I've done the legwork. My name is Tiffany Pratt, and creative projects are my lifeblood. For as long as I can remember, I have held onto my crazy ideas and worked on them until they came to life. As a child, I would hoard magazines and colored papers and pretty images in a file folder under my bed. I would obsessively write to-do and to-get lists even before I had an after-school job to afford any of it. Now, I analyze paintings in galleries to learn about colors and blending. I sit in fancy hotel lobbies, beautiful restaurants, and clients' homes to study the finishings and fabric choices. I'm thrilled when I find a new lip color in an unexpected place or a bracelet at the dollar store. The contents of others' recycling bins give me butterflies on the regular, as does the delivery of a few monthly magazines. For me, scouring through thrift stores and vintage shops is an art form and weekend garage sales are unplanned scavenger hunts where I always win. The truth is that when we get quiet enough and look around for the clues, all of the answers are waiting there for us. I am in love with life and all of the creative things that I can make and do within it. *This Can Be Beautiful* was written from my heart to inspire you to have a love affair with your heart's desires, your life, your choices, your dreams, and your things. Consider me your fairy godmother: Each page is my magic wand waving you through to make you laugh and live lighter, to motivate you, and to show you how to do it all with acceptance, love, a little effort, and a lot of hot glue.

I have worked on this philosophy my whole life. I have always allowed myself to try things at least once. I believe in experimentation and I eventually get comfortable with the impermanence of it all. I attribute my fearless style of living, decorating, dressing, celebrating, and creating to a simple phrase: *Act now, think later.* What this means to me is that you should choose wisely when you acquire, create, or make decisions and worry about the details later. What this does is hone your ability to trust your instincts and go with your gut, and it usually shows you that your first choice yields the best results. All you need to know is that you thought, "This can be beautiful," and now it is. This way of designing your life ensures that your world and everything in it will be truly one-of-a-kind and custom-made because you created it with your own two hands.

You might think that this kind of lifestyle will cost you more than just your time, but it doesn't have to be that way. I have never believed that you need a lot of money to have a fabulous life. I spent my twenties inside a very affluent community and worked as a personal shopper at Saks Fifth Avenue. Surrounded by luxury, I still constantly thought to myself, "I can make that or find it somewhere else for less money!" I was also a stone's throw away from Manhattan, where I was schooled in the art of hunting and gathering finds from stores that would often disappear overnight. Regardless of the find, I learned that if I loved it, then it was cool and it didn't matter where I had bought it, or what was on trend. My love for my found treasures trumped everything, and that love made it work in the end.

I have used this lifestyle philosophy as my own form of therapy, too. Like many of us, I have been torn apart by extreme loss and personal grief, the kind that some people never recover from. I have pulled myself through some heart-wrenching circumstances by tapping into my creativity, my art, a wild project, a garage sale watercolor kit, or a late-night furniture-painting project. By using my hands in times of crisis, I have tapped into my inner light that I have colored and glittered to make my own. And most importantly, I've realized that my ideals were not supposed to be just dreams—if I kept moving toward them, I could make them my reality. And that is what I want for you. I want to inspire you to keep moving toward your happiness, to celebrate your uniqueness, and to own your style. Life can be as beautiful or as boring as we choose. And I choose to think that it can be beautiful.

These days, I am an active designer and stylist. These broad titles mean that I can be found doing most anything creative. Whether it's decorating a private home or business; designing my canvas dress collection for makers (those who make their bucks using their own two hands); art directing for companies; shopping for wardrobes; speaking to companies on creativity; or appearing on various television shows for HGTV, I pride myself on my inventiveness. No job is too small, and everything can be one-of-a-kind. Writing this book has given me a chance to share with you some of the things that I have learned or done along my creative path. This is a collection of goodies intended to serve as a springboard for your own creativity. Let the images inspire you and make you want to try something new, possibly failing and all the while embracing the beautiful imperfection.

If all else fails, throw some glitter on it. That's what I do.

HOW THIS BOOK WORKS

I don't generally read instructions. How about you? As a creative type, I seldom agree with general conventions—I don't bake much, because I don't like to follow recipes exactly. Following rules is a little boring for me, so it's no surprise that I create pretty much the same way. I begin with the tools I know I need, I have a general idea of how to get rolling, and then I dive right in and rarely look back. Some of the best things I have made were born of happy accidents.

This Can Be Beautiful is about making your own rules and doing what feels right for you. A book written in a step-by-step fashion would completely clash with the lifestyle I lead. So, here's how I hope you will navigate this book: Start with a funny story that will entertain you, then check out the tools I suggest you'll need to create each project. You can add in extra items or subtract the things that you know you would never use. Each project will be organized by a BEGINNING, MIDDLE, and END sequence. These steps are meant to illustrate what the process will *feel* like, more than what it should *look* like. I'll share examples of where my projects end up, but yours may not look the same, which is the point.

You'll notice little diamond icons at the end of each craft intro that will give you a level of difficulty for the project. You'll also notice that there are only five "hard" projects—that is, triple diamonds—in the book. The rest are bunny hill and medium bunny hill. Me, I like to stay on the bunny hill. You'll see that beside each craft name there is an icon to tell you about how much time each project will take. And, at the end of every chapter, you'll find a workbook page. Here is where I hope you will put pen to paper and write down some ideas, plans, and sketches of your own.

Ultimately, I want every person of every skill level to feel welcomed and encouraged here. Some people subscribe to a minimal aesthetic, and you folks can stop before the second level of glitter frosting is added. Others will wonder when to stop, and they might take my ideas to the next level. Ultimately, I want my ideas to be only suggestions and inspirations that lead you on your own journey into a life created by your love and unharnessed creativity.

TIPS & TOOLS

Having the best supplies and a replica of the shelves at a craft store is not the name of the game here. I am a collector and an organizer by nature, so most of the items that I have stockpiled in my craft artillery are things that I have salvaged or reused from former projects. If you're new to the crafting scene and you need some items to get you started, select some items from the list on the following page that you think you might use most.

I recommend throughout this book that you frequent the dollar store for most of the items listed. I don't like working with things that are hard to find or expensive. I love supplies in volume and I don't want to suggest spending a premium for my wild ideas. If you need crafting tools that are more heavy-duty, I would check out your local craft, hardware, or big-box home improvement store.

All of these are the basic items you will appreciate having on-hand as we begin our journey. The more specific items that are listed in the upcoming projects will be just as affordable and easy to find.

• If you pass by a garage or yard sale, make sure to stop. You might find a score of loot in Grandma's sewing tin that could change your life. Yard sales and estate sales are filled with goodies beyond your wildest dreams.

• When you're looking for things to do in your city, check to see if there is a flea market that you can visit.

• Wear headphones if you're listening to loud music at night while painting up a storm. You do not want to upset the neighbors with your late-night muse visit.

• Stash some chocolate in your cupboard to keep the creative buzz rolling.

• Have a pile of crafting PJs or clothes ready so you don't have to paint or craft in your work-out clothes or evening attire.

• Rubber or latex gloves are good to have around. Sometimes I forget this, and then I'll have dyed purple and pink hands for a few days.

• Designate a spot or cupboard for storing all of your making supplies. It's important that you are able to see and access everything you have!

• Resealable bags are great for scraps and easy cleanup, so keep them close by.

• Crafting can lead to a bit of hoarding when it comes to having and collecting items to be stocked and ready. Know when to hold 'em and when to give 'em away. You do not want your craft cupboard to become a craft wasteland.

• Reusable drop cloths are primo. I especially like the ones with the absorbent paper top and the plastic backing. Also, a good, hearty canvas one is always a crafting classic. The canvas drop cloths can be washed, too. I like that.

• Always keep a close eye on the recycling bin. In my opinion, there are a lot of items that hit the bin that should be kept. Newspapers, toilet paper rolls, egg cartons, tin cans, cereal boxes, old tissue paper, shipping boxes, bubble wrap, any glass jars with lids, soda cans, and yogurt containers with lids (to name just a few).

• Old towels or rags are great ripped into working pieces for everyday use.

• Cotton balls and Q-tips are not just good for bathroom use. These items are amazing for crafting, detail work, and tidying things.

• Plastic shower caps can cover a working palette quickly and easily to keep your paint wet and ready for use the next day.

TOOLS

At the risk of repeating myself, if you pass by a yard sale, STOP! Really great stuff can be found that you can add to your making and crafting gear for almost no cost.

- Hot glue gun x 2: look for one industrial (bigger in size and hotter in temperature) and one regular size (smaller and runs cooler).
- Paintbrushes: I want you to have a variety. I would love you to have brushes for walls, brushes for furniture, and brushes for detail work and painting in general.
- Mod Podge (glazing glue)
- White glue
- Adhesive Velcro
- Scissors for everyday use, plus fabric scissors
- Multihead screwdriver or power drill—depending on how bad-ass you want to be
- Mortar and pestle
- Glitter: both clear and something that is micro-fiber or all the glitter (but preferably all the glitter)
- Colorful gemstones
- Straight-edge blade
- Sewing needles

- Embroidery thread
- Clothes pegs
- Sharpies in every color
- Ribbons and trims of any and every kind
- Fabric dyes in any shade
- Watercolor paints
- Acrylic paints
- Plastic or rubber washtub
- Wax paper
- Rope/yarn
- Tape measure
- Latex spray paints in your favorite shades
- Safety pins
- Confetti
- Chalk pastels
- Colored and clear tape of any kind

EVERY DAY IS
EVER DAZZLING

A change of perspective and a bag of crafting supplies is what to pack for this journey to your new *This Can Be Beautiful* lifestyle. A fresh eye and a new way of thinking and seeing are soon going to make your everyday life dazzling. Somewhere within the beautiful disarray of your life is everything you need to reimagine what you already have. Old can be new and new can be blissfully strange and wonderfully interesting. Start with this: If you see something you love—a color or a fabric—stop worrying about what other people might think and instead notice how it makes you feel. Owning what makes you happy is one of the best secrets I can share when you begin to make your everyday every bit as wonderful as you want it to be.

As you move through the items in your life, think about the energy you transfer over to them, simply through your thoughts and touch. Whether it's brushing your fingers through a closed rose to spread out the petals, positioning the pillows in a new way on your bed, rearranging the dishes on the shelf to show off your new teacup, or adding a new plant to the kitchen windowsill . . . All of these little yet magical things make a difference. Sometimes all it takes is adding or subtracting something small in your life for it to feel new again. The changes you can create around an object, an outfit, or a room just by engaging with it and renewing its energy are miraculous! Don't be afraid to put your hands all over your life. Your furniture, your light switches, your windowsills . . . Your day-to-day life is simply a vessel for your conscious love.

Open the doors inside yourself and your life.

Things are about to get beautifully messy.

LIGHT SWITCH FACELIFT

For most people, the typical, plain, plastic light switch covers adorn the walls of every room in their home. I have spent many years looking at and removing those light switch covers—either to paint the walls or just to give those covers a facelift with some pretty papers. I rarely replace them on the wall in the same simple format that I removed them. As a fun weekend activity for you, your gal pals, or all the neighborhood kids, take them all down and put them in the hands of greatness. If you offer up a pretty selection of things to stick to them, the results cannot be beat. The best news is that if you ever want the white plain-Jane covers back one day, they cost less than a dollar at the hardware store. Win! **LEVEL** ◆◆◆

THE LINE-UP

- Mod Podge (matte or shiny)
- Clear glitter
- Tissue paper squares, fabric, wallpaper, or all of the above!
- Sponge brushes

FYI

If you don't have tissue paper or tissue paper shapes, you can use magazines, confetti, newspaper, fabric, or wallpaper samples instead! Anything that you like will look the best in your space.

THE BEGINNING Unscrew all of the light switch covers and tape the screws onto the back sides. This way it will be easy to reinstall them later. Lay out the Mod Podge and glitter in easy-to-access bowls and have confetti, tissue paper squares, fabric, and wallpaper all cut to your preferred sizes. Give your light switch covers a wipe down and get rocking!

QUICK TRICK

If you don't have Mod Podge, have no fear! If you add a few drops of food coloring to regular white glue and mix it in, it turns into a pastel-tinted dream sure to dry into a nice hue.

THE MIDDLE Each light switch cover should start by being totally covered in Mod Podge. Once that's done, layer the tissue paper squares everywhere and remember: There are no rules here or design concepts to follow. The most important thing to note is that you need to Mod Podge overtop of your tissue once you have covered the surface with the glued-down tissue.

THE END All of your light switches are complete. You've brushed Mod Podge on the top of all of them to seal your creations down and you've dusted clear glitter on top of the wet Mod Podge to make your lighting covers spectacularly glittery. Lay them flat to dry overnight and put them back in place in the morning.

BIG FURNITURE PAINT-UP

Sometimes the big pink elephant in your room is the piece of furniture that needs a paint job. That one huge thing that you think should never be painted is probably the one thing that should be. Breaking the rules and trying things that people think are bad ideas is usually the most thrilling approach and generally yields the best results. Don't overthink it. Choose a "pop" color or a gallon of bright white paint and just start. It's amazing how much an exciting paint job can invigorate a space and get your blood racing. LEVEL ◆◆◆

THE LINE-UP

- Medium grit sandpaper
- Drop cloth
- Painter's tape
- 1 gallon of paint in the color and finish of your choice!
- Yogurt container
- 2.5-inch paintbrush
- Paint tray
- Foam roller
- Cloth rag

TAKING THE PLUNGE

When you're tackling something huge there's always a thought that you won't do it right or that it'll turn out looking bad. Stop the negative self-talk and start the project.

THE BEGINNING You've emptied the piece of furniture you're about to paint. You've vacuumed it to remove old dirt and dust. You've sanded and wiped it down to prepare the surface for painting. Now lay the drop cloth under it, open the windows, and apply painter's tape to the places and edges that require covering. Pour the paint into a yogurt container for the brush cutting and have the foam roller and a tray of paint at the ready. Turn up the music! It's showtime!

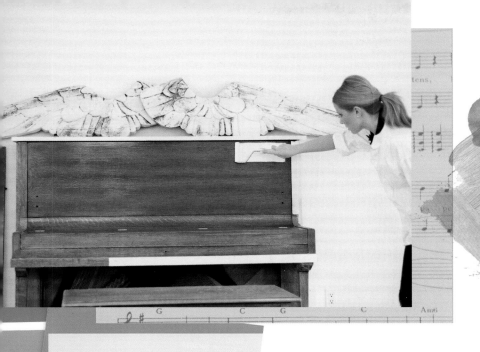

NOTE
If you play really loud music and allow yourself to zone out, this type of painting goes quickly and becomes addictive and therapeutic.

THE MIDDLE You have succumbed to the Zen meditative quality that is painting and you start thinking, "Why didn't I do this earlier?" Although the piece is currently a work in progress, you can now see how good it's going to look. Take your time, and remember that there is a limit to what you can accomplish in a day. You might not get this done all at once, but make sure to finish it the next day if you let it dry overnight. We do not want painting procrastination to set in.

THE END It's always good to let paint dry and settle overnight to see if another coat is necessary before you wrap everything up. Once you're happy with the look of your furniture, consider it a job well done. Rinse your brushes, remove the painter's tape, and take a really long shower to scrub the paint off your arms. Place the piece of furniture back in its rightful spot and suddenly your space feels like a dream. You did it!

PILLOWCASE CLUTCH

You know those pillowcases lying around destined for the rag pile? Perhaps the pillowcases in a print that even your grandma might find dated? Well, I want 'em. They will soon be the pillow-talk of the town . . . in bag form! These worked-in fabric treasures are the perfect carry-all clutches for tinier lady evening items or as laptop holders. In a few easy sewing or hot glue gun moves, you can have one or five of these in your life.

LEVEL ◆◆◆

THE LINE-UP

- Sewing machine (if you have it)
- Pillowcase
- Needle and thread
- Hot glue gun
- Fabric scissors
- Tea towel
- Oversized button
- Self-adhesive Velcro

NOTE

I've added a tea towel to your supplies list. If you layer your pillowcase on top of a tea towel, you'll have a clutch with a nice soft liner that is extra thick and will stand up a little better to the wear and tear of your beautiful life.

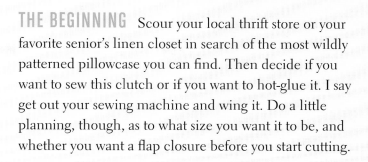

THE BEGINNING Scour your local thrift store or your favorite senior's linen closet in search of the most wildly patterned pillowcase you can find. Then decide if you want to sew this clutch or if you want to hot-glue it. I say get out your sewing machine and wing it. Do a little planning, though, as to what size you want it to be, and whether you want a flap closure before you start cutting.

HOT ALTERNATIVE

If you don't want to sew this clutch, all you need to do is hot-glue the edges where you would be sewing. Fold over the raw edges of the fabric and glue them down. Now you're in business . . . the hot-gluing business.

THE MIDDLE Cut your pillowcase to size and sew or hot-glue in the tea towel liner. Make sure your hot glue gun is really hot! If you decided to sew the clutch, you'll only need the hot glue to attach the button and the Velcro. Just glue on the Velcro where you want the closure to be—underneath the flap or in between the two fabric halves.

THE END It's time to stuff the clutch with your laptop or your lady bits and bobs. You have the remnants all over and you should feel proud of how awesome of a sewer/gluer you are. This has inspired you to think of more reasons to pull out the sewing machine or find more people to make these quick-sew clutches for. Booya!

<1HR

CONFESSION

This idea came to me when I wanted to make use of the last few clear furniture pads that I had left over from padding the drawers of a dresser. The leftovers percolated in my head till this idea surfaced!

FURNITURE PAD STUDS

Every time I see clear furniture stick-on pads I think of buying a bunch, bedazzling them, and turning them into a MAJOR 80s stick-on earring collection! One that I would have coveted when I was a kid—or maybe one that I would covet now. They have a great texture and the nice adhesive backing ensures that they really stay on. Best of all, even in the wildest of circumstances, if you lose your earrings, it's NBD—you can just glitter up another round. LEVEL ◆◇◇

THE LINE-UP

• Small adhesive bindis or gems (you can use whatever you think would be cool)
• Glitter of any kind
• Clear nail polish
• Small clear plastic furniture pads

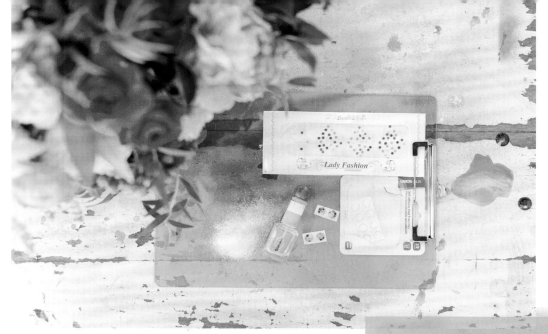

THE BEGINNING With the cheap $3.00 bindi collection that you scored from a Little India visit, you have the inspiration for the polka dot earring pattern of your dreams! Pull out the glitter and your clear nail polish, because it is time to adorn these babies.

THE MIDDLE Bindis often have a little adhesive on the back, so it's easy to stick them on the furniture pads. Each earring does not need to be an exact replica of the others, so mix it up. Having two similar earrings is way cooler than having two identical earrings.

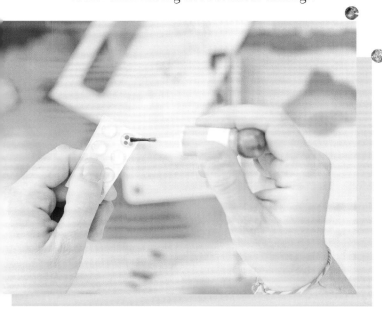

THE END Once the bindis are attached to the furniture pads, go over them with a nice thick coat of clear nail polish and layer a coat of clear glitter on top of the wet polish for sparkle. These take no time to make and look so cute! Make a batch and give them out to your gal pals. You'll see these earrings become the talk of the group text!

PUNCH BOWL SPRAY-OUT

<1HR

My mother made a "take your pants off" sangria for my sister's wedding shower many years ago and filled up a plastic punch bowl with her concoction. Not being much of a drinking woman, I was more focused on the fact that my mother could have presented this master blend in a far more inviting way. Here I have an idea that can be used on both plastic and glass punch bowl sets and will surely bring life to not only the party but also the snack table! I promise that once you see this misted, candy-colored dream, you will not turn back or regret your spraying decision. LEVEL ◆◆◆

THE LINE-UP
• Punch bowl and glasses
• Drop cloth
• As many colors of latex spray paint as you want (I'm a fan of a matte finish)
• Clear coat spray paint
• Paper towel

FYI
This craft idea is a study in impermanence. The color may eventually wash off, but you can spray the bowl a few different colors and it will develop a beautiful patina over time.

THE BEGINNING You've washed all of your glassware and laid out the drop cloth. Place the punch bowl and any glasses that come with the set upside down on the drop cloth. Start shaking all of the spray paint cans in preparation for the big spray.

THE MIDDLE You might be stumped about mixing paint colors or wondering if you should just commit to one color. I'd like to remind you to go with your gut and to have some fun with this. The objective here is to dazzle your guests and to play up a once-plain piece. Remember: Be bold! Be punchy! Start with the bottom of the bowl and work your way up the sides.

THE END You've finished spraying your glassware and now you should let it dry overnight. I recommend that you put a shiny coat of clear spray paint on top of the glass if you love the results and want them around for a few washes—and handwashing is key. Otherwise, leave it without a top coat so that the paint will come off over time and you can layer the color as needed. This is my favorite part about art and crafting—seeing what happens if you experiment with different colors.

TIP

Only mist the bottoms of each piece of glassware.
The paint will lightly spread down the sides,
but the rims should remain unsprayed so that
no one will ingest the paint in any way.
Also, the look ends up appearing like ombré.

STRING CURTAIN

Maybe I should have been a hippie or at least been born during a time when front doors were the only ones necessary for a home. When I dreamed up this string curtain, I was in need of a covering for a doorway on the cheap and wanted to use what I had hanging around in excess. Using all of the neon string from the hardware store that I had over-purchased and a leftover cardboard tube from a roll of fabric, I was able to quickly fashion this and make something filled with all the vibes of a true peace and love–filled hippie home.

LEVEL ◆◆◆

SHARP TIP

Fabric scissors are a wonderful investment piece for every craft cupboard. Although no fabric is used in this craft, having a nice sharp pair of scissors to cut with is very helpful.

THE BEGINNING Get your cardboard tube out and hold it up to the doorway that you want to cover. Then cut it to that width with a straight-edge blade. Using the shortcut to measuring, drop the string from the top of the door to the floor, and then double up that length and start cutting your pieces of string. Keep cutting until you have enough string to cover your door. The string cutting for this project is the most time-consuming work here. Try to be accurate so that you don't waste too much string.

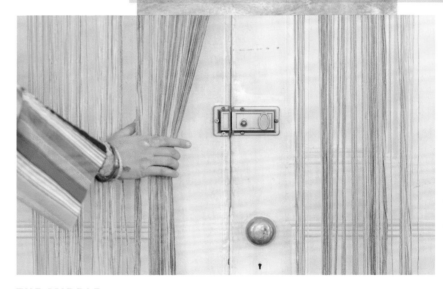

THE MIDDLE Fold the string over so it's doubled up, then wrap the doubled string over the cardboard tube and feed the string through the top loop. Repeat until you have tightly covered the length of the cardboard tube. This step can take some time and may require the playing of your favorite music or the watching of your favorite movie on a loop.

THE END You have totally covered the cardboard tube with the neon string. All that's left is to attach two end caps on the tube, so pull out the duct tape. But before you tape over the ends, run any leftover string through the tube so it dangles out both ends. Cover the ends of the tube with the duct tape, leaving a bit of room for the end strings to flow out. Tie the end strings together at the top of the tube and let the curtain hang over the doorway.

ON REPEAT

When I'm creating, I want to listen to the same music or watch the same movie over and over again until the project is completed. I wanted to share that little habit I have, so you know you're not alone if you do it too.

INSPIRATIONS FROM THIS CHAPTER ARE:

_____
_____
_____
_____
_____
_____
_____
_____
_____
_____
_____
_____
_____
_____
_____
_____
_____

HOME
IS WHERE THE
GLITTER IS

OH
LA
LA

I had a secret love affair with home décor until I was put to task renovating an old home in Connecticut. From painting, spackling, and wallpapering to reupholstering and restoring, I built a home that was one-of-a-kind. My affinity for it was a clue that this was something I should consider doing in my life. Curating perfect, individualized spaces for my clients is truly one of my favorite things to do. I love to outfit homes in textures and beauty while making them more functional and organized than they ever were before. I realize that not everyone can translate their ideas about interiors from dream to reality, but with some experimentation and time, your space will start taking the shape of your dreams. Your living quarters should evoke your five senses and activate all that makes you feel at home. What does it smell like? What are you hearing? What are you seeing? What are you feeling? I can almost taste the chocolate.

I believe that a space can be your soul made visible. I believe that both our way of life and the area that surrounds us can be transformative elements for our well-being, creativity, and self-expression—in short, our living spaces have a magical power over us. My home, fondly referred to as the Glitter Suite, is my center. It's my haven, my studio, and my self fully realized within four walls. Simple changes can be a catalyst for real transformation, and I have tweaked and made tiny changes to my space over time that have resulted in my own personal nirvana. Don't think of external things that you need in order to fill the space "just because."

Rather, look around at what you have and think about how you can make existing items better by painting, gluing, or redoing them. Invention is born of necessity, and some of my most exciting décor ideas occurred when I didn't have much but did much with what I had.

Before you journey through the nooks and crannies of your life, remember that it's more important to love something than to have it in your home. If you don't have some kind of love affair with every little thing in your home, then think of someone who will and give it away to them to make space for a more energetic area around you. Also, clean and tidy spaces are the most pleasant. When you think of creative crafting and DIY projects, you may not always think of cleaning—but I promise that the two are intertwined and that a simple and uncluttered home is a powerful way to spread peace, love, and order throughout each room. In this chapter, I share ideas that will assist in the organization, style, function, and movement of a space. These concepts are fun, playful, and easy on the budget on purpose. I've created them to ensure that you'll find at least one thing that can bring a Zen zing to your home and a big OM to your heart.

If home is where the heart is, then let's go put love on everything!

TIE-DYE YOUR OLD SHEETS!

2+ HRS

I have a deep love for things that are multipurpose. Sheets can be curtains, tablecloths, and forts. There is really no end to the things that I can do with a good quality sheet. Even with a good sheet, though, discoloration can happen after a while. But I've got a good idea for what to do next, and it's called fabric tie-dye. Color triumphs over questionable stains every time. Let's give your old sheets a second chance at life by tie-dying them into some kind of wavy and wild dream! If you won't put them on the bed they can be repurposed once they are colored up! Check it out. **LEVEL** ◆◆◆

THE LINE-UP

- Old bed sheets and pillowcases
- Tie-dye kit
- Rubber gloves
- Drop cloth
- Elastic bands
- Washer & dryer
- A few sink-sized rubber bins

THE BEGINNING After a big laundry session you realize that your sheets are not the bright white crisp darlings that you once brought home from the linen store. But with a quick trip to the craft store for a tie-dye kit, you will solve all of your linen closet woes with some bright, happy colors and patterns. Get your gloves on—it's time to start mixing! The first step is to lay out your drop cloth, then to mix all the dyes in the bottles that come with the kit. Every kit of tie dye is different, so please read and follow the instructions on the back of your kit so you know how to prepare your dye.

THE MIDDLE Once the dyes are all mixed, you are faced with one big question: Do I make elastic ring patterns all over my sheets or do I just shake the dye randomly all over? I think that it's a good idea to shake the dye all over to have a splashed and sprinkled effect. This process goes really fast and is way more fun that you ever remembered from your crafting camp days. Once this is all done and every square inch of your pillowcases and top and fitted sheets are sprinkled, let the dye sit for an hour to set in the rubber bins.

FYI

You don't need to dye your sheets in a tie-dye style; you can opt for a more basic solid dye job by using simple fabric dyes that can be added to your sheets in the washing machine. This is another easy way to freshen your sheets.

THE END Now you're ready to take your sheets to the washer and dryer. If you've added elastics to the sheets, take them off. Fire up the washer with cold water and then throw the sheets in the dryer when they're done. Once the sheets are dry, race to put them on your bed to see the Technicolor goodness that you've created.

HOUSE NUMEROLOGY

When numbers coincide with a crafting event, it adds up to good times and good vibes for both you and your home. I judge a home by how relatively cool the number is—TRUTH! When your house number is on point, it sets the tone for the rest of the home to be one fascinating decision after another. This is a good place to decide how you want to come off as both a neighbor and style siren in your 'hood. And remember: This is your house, your style, your vibes, and your color scheme. Use my process below as a guideline for launching your own concept. Now, let's get adding! **LEVEL** ◆◆

THE LINE-UP

- **Your existing house numbers**
- Screwdriver
- Hot glue gun
- Gemstones
- Glitter
- Rhinestones and/or old costume jewelry
- Ribbon
- Clear coat spray paint

THE BEGINNING You decided that you're done putting baby in the corner and it's time for your house numbers to have their rise to neighborly fame! With a simple screwdriver to remove the numbers and a fired-up glue gun, you're well on your way to showing off your true numbers. If you have a jar filled with bits and bobs and a few ribbons, you can cover these numbers to perfection in no time flat.

THE MIDDLE You've realized that the word "encrusted" means a lot to you in this moment. With the hot glue gun at your side, you can layer up all the small, medium, and large pretty pieces. The world is your oyster here! Make the numbers your own. If you do not dig what I have put together for my numbers, take a spin of your own and dazzle your digits your way. The idea here is that you make the numbers add up to YOU!

THE END Once your numbers are dazzling, you're ready to seal them in a divine layer of clear coat to preserve your handiwork from the elements. Let 'em dry overnight and call your neighbor over for the big reveal in the morning. Tell her that no coffee is required—these numbers will leave her with a whole new kind of buzz.

NOTE

If you're one of the lucky folks who had already installed cool black-and-white wallpaper long before you read this book, you're ahead of the game! Just grab your markers and start coloring!

WALLPAPER COLOR-IN

2+ HRS

One thing that I have done my whole life is color. A family tradition that has always prevailed in our house revolves around the use of coloring books, markers, and deep chats. My mother brings coloring books to our family gatherings to ensure that everyone hunkers down at a table to chat and color in the lines together. With all of the very hip and cool black-and-white wallpaper options on the market right now, I cannot help but be inspired by my mother and all of those years of staring at the black-and-white lined designs. This little DIY is for the people who may have already wallpapered their walls in a black-and-white pattern but are looking for more color, or for people who want to hunt out the paper and color it in from the get-go! This project is like installing the biggest coloring book you have ever seen and making it your own with some permanent markers and some time. **LEVEL** ◆◆◆

THE LINE-UP
- Black-and-white wallpaper of your choice
- Wallpaper glue (if the paper you've chosen is not pre-pasted)
- Straight-edge blade (to cut the wallpaper)
- Squeegee
- Sharpie markers in various colors

THE BEGINNING
If you've never hung wallpaper before, jump on YouTube or call your local wallpaper installer for some tips. You got this. If the wallpaper that you chose is pre-pasted, this will make installation easy! Take your time, don't rush, and do a good job of getting that paper up! If you don't, you'll be staring at the lines and bumps that don't match up.

THE MIDDLE
Once the paper is up, grab your Sharpies and start to color in the lines. This is like filling in the biggest coloring book of your life. I like the idea of white space. If you do too, you'll want to think about leaving a lot of white space around the areas that you're coloring. As well, choose Sharpies in colors that you want to incorporate in the room. This is a really subtle and fun way to bring these shades into the room. Is it not the most freeing thing in the world to color on your walls?

THE END
You have colored in random designs all over this wallpaper and nobody would even know that you did this with a Sharpie! Keep in mind that with such a dramatic wallpaper idea it's best to balance out the rest of the room with simple white walls. Now move your furniture back into place and get your sister to come over and fawn over this amazing project.

1+ HR

SCRAP FABRIC CURTAIN

I'm a sucker for textures and reusable items. It's actually my life's mission to make the mundane insanely desirable. Let me show you how to make a textural curtain delight with some scrap fabric, string, and time. That's the thing about a maker's life—we might not have time for grocery shopping, but we can sure make time to rip some strips of fabric and tie them on a string for curtains in the living room. This project is a meditative and therapeutic one that is too easy to make. The best part about this concept is that although the strips of fabric allow for some privacy, they're still not a solid piece of fabric, so light can come shining through! **LEVEL** ◆◆◆

THE LINE-UP
- Scrap fabric
- Good fabric scissors
- Thick cotton string
- Two wall hooks

THE BEGINNING You've saved loads of scrap fabric from when your gal pal made you a beautiful summer dress and you've not known what to do with this surplus of beautiful fabric until now. The window in your living room has the most brilliant light pouring through it in the morning and you don't want to cover it, but you need a little privacy too. The solution? Get ripping and cutting this scrap fabric to the height of the window.

THE MIDDLE Once all of your strips have been cut to the height of the window you're covering, you'll need to tie them across a thick cotton string the same length as your window. This truly takes no time at all, and you'll find it goes quicker than you would think. Just make sure to tie the knots at the top in a nice, neat way.

IDEA
If you want some variety, you can run to the fabric store and buy a yard or two of a few contrasting fabrics to offset what you have on-hand. This way, you can pull in some alternative colors in the room and give this window dressing some dimension.

THE END Once the scrap fabric strips have been neatly tied to the length of the cotton string, all you need are two hooks to install on either side of the window. Once they're installed, you can wrap the string around the hook on one side and then pull tightly and wrap the other side of the string to pull the fabric curtain tight across the window. This style of curtain is very bohemian and incredibly textural, sure to bring both light and privacy to your space!

MEDITATION
Repeated actions have a meditative quality. This is why I love showering, doing dishes, and driving. Treat this project like a mental retreat and you will imbue this entire piece with your good vibes and peaceful mind.

THE LINE-UP

- Pegboard cut to a size that will fit your door
- Hooks for the pegboard
- 1 quart of wall paint in a color of your choice
- Foam roller
- Zip ties
- Spray paint in a color of your choice
- Drop cloth
- Over-the-door hanging hooks
- 8 recycled soda cans
- Can opener
- Hole punch
- Hot glue gun
- Ribbon
- Scissors
- Small mirror

MIRROR CADDY (on the door)

2+ HRS

When I was in high school, I had a really small bedroom. My queen-sized bed took up almost the entire space. And when I recently created this caddy featuring storage cans and a mirror, I realized that this caddy is made of things I could have easily gotten my hands on and it would have made my teenage life and primping a breeze! This project is designed for small spaces and is perfect for accessing little items and storing things in a nice and neat way. Forget about Mirror, Mirror on the Wall. Let's embrace Mirror, Mirror on the Door! LEVEL ◆◆◆

ESSENTIAL MEASURES

Never leave the house without your tape measure. You never know when you're going to need it. And also remember that you'll need a vehicle with cargo space that's large enough to fit the pegboard. Don't show up to the hardware store on your bike!

THE BEGINNING Before you head out to the hardware store to get your paint and pegboard, make sure to measure the door that you're working with so that you get the right length and width of pegboard cut. You can ask the folks at the hardware store to cut the pegboard to size for you right on the spot! While you're there, get the hooks for the pegboard, paint color you want, some paint rollers, zip ties, spray paint, drop cloth, and the door hooks. When you get home, all you'll need to do is clean out the empty cans and get painting.

THE MIDDLE Get your drop cloth laid out so you can place your pegboard and tin cans on top. Paint the pegboard using your foam roller and spray paint the empty cans. Once you're happy with the look, take a can opener and remove the tops of the soda cans. Then grab a hole punch and punch holes in the side of the cans so that the pegboard hooks can fit inside. Get your glue gun out and carefully run a line of glue around the cut-open tops of the cans. Lay your ribbon overtop of the glue so that all the sharp edges are covered. Now grab your door hooks and place them over your door. Run the zip ties through the top holes of the pegboard and hang it from the door hooks. It sounds complicated, but is so easy! All you have to do now is get the cans on and stock up your caddy.

THE END Once the pegboard is hanging from the door hooks, you're ready to get it all stocked up! Take your adorned soda cans, place the hooks through the holes, and then attach them to the bottom half of the pegboard. Attach only as many cans as you'll need to house the stuff you need to store. For the final piece, add a hook to the top of the pegboard, attach a zip tie to the mirror, and hang the mirror on the top half of the board like a vanity. This do-it-all caddy is all ready to go.

FYI
Other fun uses for soda cans can be found on page 76. Jump ahead for more inspiration!

RUG SPRAY-OUT

<1HR

I adore paint in every variety I can get it. I love the idea of coloring the world with something so accessible and easy to use. I like to have paint on my person like a tattoo artist proudly displays their ink, but instead of it being on my skin, it's on my clothes, my hands, my hair, and my shoes. But with this project, I've reached a new level of love. I'm putting paint where no man has painted before: The RUG! Plain rugs are a thing of the past and adding more texture is where it's at. Be adventurous, be wild, and be paint-filled on this new adventure. Even an old rug can be new again. This old rug is gonna look rad! LEVEL ◆◇◇

THE LINE-UP
- Cleaned-up cotton rug
- Painter's tape
- A can of latex spray paint in the color of your choice

THE BEGINNING You have a lovely cotton striped hallway runner that has seen better days. The carpet itself is not old but because of the ivory white background, it looks dirty and played. If you've thrown the carpet in for a quick wash and there are still a few dirty marks that won't come out, don't fear! Get yourself to a well-ventilated area and start to place painter's tape in patterns all over the carpet.

THE MIDDLE Once the patterns and tape are laid out on the carpet, grab the spray paint and do a light mist of color all over the rug. Focus the color and give it dimension in some areas by solidly spraying some parts. Once you've covered the rug, let it dry for about 30 minutes.

THE END Now that the spray paint is dry, take off all of the painter's tape and reveal the spray-painted haze of color over this newly revived rug! It's a showstopper and ready for the floor. The little makeover for this hall runner took no time but made an instant impact on the overall look and feeling of the hallway. BINGO!

DIVE DEEP

Painting and stenciling a big wool rug was one of my biggest harebrained schemes one winter and was the inspiration for this craft. I committed to this wild idea for a client and pumped it up way too much to back out. This is the truth about crafting, making, and creating. Most of the time, we have no idea how things will end up. We just need to commit to finishing and hope it looks as awesome in real life as it does in our dreamed-up version. Do your best, think through the variables, and keep rolling. Really cool, amazing shit will happen. Like a painted rug.

THINGS THAT I WANT TO CREATE IN MY HOME ARE:

FASHION
PLATE

When I was asked what I wanted to be when I grew up, the answer was always fashion designer. Even before I was a teenager, I pored over fashion magazines while waiting for *Fashion Television* to start. It was a language that I immediately understood. I never cared if I stood out or if what I did or wore was uncool. I was fine with it if that meant being cutting edge. Somehow being different meant more to me than anything else. And somewhere along the way, my simple ginger hair became an orange rainbow.

But behind this orange-haired character is a woman who used to curate wardrobes for the elite society of Connecticut. Picture me then with strawberry blonde hair, in a black power suit and pumps, and you'll start to imagine how it all began. On a train ride from Queens, NY, to Greenwich, CT, I was approached by a woman who ran the Fifth Avenue Club at Saks in Connecticut. She couldn't resist complimenting my coat. It was a rusty gold and cream houndstooth swing jacket with big gold buttons. It looked like Chanel and it matched my strawberry blonde bob to boot. We talked for the remainder of the ride and exchanged numbers. Soon I was the youngest, newest member of the Fifth Avenue Club and was responsible for dressing ritzy women in the latest-and-greatest designers. This time of my life was the most incredible education, and by the end, it felt like I'd gotten a degree in style from Saks.

I look at personal style like a religion. This may sound extreme, but to me, style is something that comes from the depth of your soul and is something you come back to, over and over again, like a daily mantra or prayer. This mantra can change based on your feelings or needs at a particular time or day, but nonetheless, the way you dress is a way of communicating your vibe, your style, or your prayer to the world.

Fashion and how you cover the human figure is an art form that should be both fun and inventive. The more adventures and risks you take, the more "YOU" your style becomes. Don't worry too much about trends or take fashion too seriously. Fashion and style are only one part of the game—hunting, gathering, acquiring, and sourcing are others. In this chapter, I want to blow the lid off limited style beliefs and get you to think outside your closet. I want you to begin dressing for your life like you're writing a colorful mantra for your heart and soul to say every day. The world will hear and see it as you walk down the street—and the world will smile.

Throughout this chapter, I will ask you to do things that you may not have thought to do before. What works for me may not work for you, but I hope that my suggestions and tips make it into your closet or into your heart. Please seek adventure when dressing and remember: More is more, less is less, and nothing is uncool if you love it.

Okay!
Now it's time
to play dress-up!

JUST BLEACH IT!

THE LINE-UP

- Clothing that you want to splatter
- Drop cloth
- Latex gloves
- A small bottle of bleach
- Fabric dye in your choice of color
- Small bowls
- Cotton swabs

When I was growing up, my mother had a killer skill for bleaching my clothes. And not just any clothes, but those coveted, go-to overalls that I wore all the time and those tops that were perfect in every way. When I would unfold the clothes from the Clean Pile, my mother's mishandling of chemicals would be revealed and a feeling of great loss would overcome me. This skill of hers pushed me to take over my own laundry and forced me to think quickly about how to make those bleach stains work. Now, at 36, I look for clothes that I can double-stain with bleach and colored dye, and I thank my lucky stars that my mother was such a Javex-happy laundress.

LEVEL ◆◆

THE BEGINNING It's early, you're in your PJs, and you've woken up with a hunger to craft. So you go scouring through your closet for a garment to transform. Once you've found a clean piece of clothing that you want to turn into a speckled dream, lay it out on a drop cloth or on top of your washing machine. Put your latex gloves on and pour the bleach into a small bowl. Then place your fingertips in the bowl and begin dripping and flicking the bleach strategically on top of the garment. Let it sit for an hour, then throw it in the washing machine.

REMEMBER

We all make mistakes when doing laundry, but these are the times when a bleach accident turns into a perfect chance to splatter the whole thing since the damage is done.

THE MIDDLE Once the wash is done, pull out your garment and lay it out on a drop cloth or towel to begin the next step: adding color to your bleach speckles. Pour the dye that you've chosen into little bowls and put your gloves back on. You can add a little water to the dye to dilute the color if you want it lighter. You might be immediately reminded of the sugar candy dots that you used to crave from the corner store when you were younger. Dip your cotton swabs into the little bowls of dye and start candy-dotting colors on top of the bleach speckles. Once you've added the color where you want it, let the dye set for a few hours.

THE END Once the dye is set, wash and dry the garment one more time. If you pull it out of the dryer and all you can think about is dyeing a pair of fabric pumps to make matching shoes, know that I support this idea. Head back to the dye bowls and work on your shoes! Everybody loves a good matching outfit set!

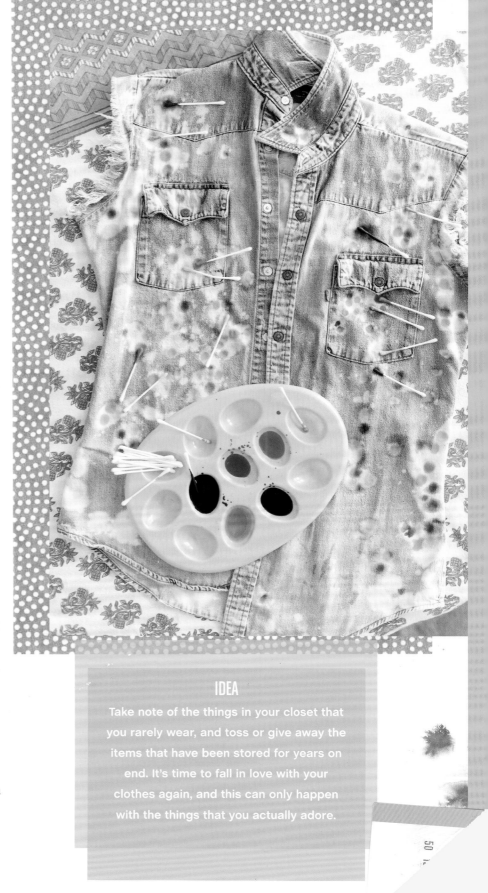

IDEA

Take note of the things in your closet that you rarely wear, and toss or give away the items that have been stored for years on end. It's time to fall in love with your clothes again, and this can only happen with the things that you actually adore.

ROSE-ARTY RINGS

I have always had a strange fascination with icing roses. They are so simple and classic, yet so "grandma" and hokey. How could I NOT be intrigued? They are practically everything I stand for. They remind me of Wanda, my Gramie, who hardly ever baked but had a pair of earrings, a bracelet, a ring, and a necklace to match every outfit. You wonder where I get my OCD, bed-making, never-cooking, color-coordinating ways? Wanda. She also had baby blue roses all over her home and, if she baked at all, it was only ginger cookies. She once sent me a package of ginger cookies to share with my sisters, but I ate the whole thing. I kept this a secret for years until Wanda eventually blew my cover. I should have made it up to her by buying her a vanilla cake with blue icing roses on it. So, in my Gramie's honor, and to beg her forgiveness by way of craft, I have created the rose-arty ring. Edible and breakable jewelry to match most of your outfits, and filled with the kind of hokey-chic vibe that Wanda would have loved and that you will go sugar-crazy for! LEVEL ◆◆◆

THE LINE-UP
- 6 icing roses (buy them at the local bulk food store or grocery store)
- Hot glue gun
- Unadorned adjustable rings

THE BEGINNING Start scouring the local bulk food store for icing roses. You might scream with delight and try to grab them all, until the quiet stock boy asks you what you're planning on doing with 50 icing roses. Now you realize you don't need them all. Even if you were Liberace, you'd only need 10. So, settle for a few less roses in assorted sizes and colors. Cheap and thrilling—that's another of my mantras, by the way. Head home to find your hot glue gun and the rings to glue them on.

THE MIDDLE Once the hot glue is warmed up, you can begin feverishly gluing icing roses to the tops of your ring bases. This takes no time. You have barely started Liberace's "Moonlight Sonata" and the rings are heading to the drying rack for the night. Now head to the closet to start planning an outfit to match.

REALIZATION

Sharing is caring. You may have a blush-colored sweater that will show off your rose-arty rings, but you have at least five rose-arty rings that you can pass out to your peeps. A spontaneous crafting gift to your bestie is truly un-selfie. Fold those rings into some tissue and pass them out.

THE END Roses are red; violets are blue; making icing rose rings is cray cray, but I still love you.

GLITTER HO-SIERY

<1HR

Some people think I'm a glitter ho. I like to think of myself more as a glitter pusher. I spring glitter on people who say they don't want glitter around them—until I arrive, and suddenly they're okay that some part of their body has glitter on it. Take my business cards, for example. They're little square cards inside of tiny plastic bags, stuffed with glitter. You have to open up the bag and rescue the card from the glitter to get my details. This also means that your finger or hand will have glitter on it, and then that glitter spreads to other things, and then . . . you cannot get me out of your mind. This example leads me to the top dog of my glitter-pushing agenda: my glitter ho-siery. Your legs will shine so bright and leave a trail of glitter magic behind you so that nobody will even care about your dress. LEVEL ◆◆◆

THE LINE-UP

- Pantyhose in the color of your choice
- Aloe vera gel
- Super-fine glitter in a color of your choice

REMEMBER

It is more fun to craft with your clothes than with your credit card. Change your brain from *What can I buy?* to *What can I bling?* You will find your wardrobe will be more fun and in turn you will have more FUN-DS.

THE BEGINNING You're headed out on a magical date and you want to wear something fabulous, shimmering, and unique, but nothing in your closet fits the bill. Get yourself to the drugstore for some pantyhose and aloe vera gel. Not what you would expect, but a game changer, nonetheless. When you return, take a bath and then put on your standby little pink dress and your new pantyhose.

THE MIDDLE Do your makeup now, because the next step to your outfit adornments may take over, so you need to be totally ready. If you suddenly have an urge to turn on Katy Perry, do so. The final act of this getting-ready story means covering your hose-clad legs in aloe vera gel, then layering glitter on top. All of a sudden, your little pink dress gets a sprinkling of pixie dust and your legs start shimmering like a princess costume from Costco. It takes courage to rock something crafty and over the top. Listen to Katy Perry for a few songs to get up the vibes before you step out of the house. As well, know that anything or anyone you come in contact with from this point on will be covered in glitter, so tonight is your night to be Tinkerbell—but to be on the safe side, wash your hands before you head out.

THE END You've sprinkled your car, your boyfriend's couch, the local hot spot, and every sidewalk in between with your glittery fairy dust. This glitter ho-siery can turn some heads and game-change an outfit and your way of life. You also may have realized that this is an accessory that you will need to try out for a night on the dance floor. As well, this is a concept that your boyfriend will never let you live down because his sectional is now shimmering for life.

OFF THE CUFF

THE LINE-UP
- Toilet paper rolls
- Ribbons
- Scissors
- Hot glue gun
- Rhinestones
- Grandma's old costume jewelry

There are a few accessories that I cannot dress without, and bangles and bracelets are some of them. Earrings and necklaces are hit-and-miss for me, but bracelets are life-changing. I love layering them. I love mixing all different materials of bangle together. And I love spending NO money on them and maxing them out on my arm. One day when I was in the bathroom, I realized that the empty toilet paper roll was the lowest I could go. Literally and figuratively. I figured that if I could make a stellar cuff out of a toilet paper roll, I would have really reached cheapie cuff nirvana. So I set out on my mission to fill my arm with cheap fabulousness and I am here to tell you I have returned a hero. Friends, I have designed a cuff that you would never know was cardboard roll under all that TP ("TP" is for "toilet paper"!). Drab to Fab anyone? YES! LEVEL

THE BEGINNING You have asked the lady who lives below you to stop watching late-night television so loudly and to save you all her toilet paper rolls. This is a good tactic as she probably never leaves the house and she pees a lot. (I like trying crafts with multiple backups because it gives me chances to try different designs, make extra as gifts, and mess up!) Collect them by the end of the week from your kind downstairs neighbor and settle into your Friday night with a gluten-free pepperoni pizza, and all your craft supplies. Turn on the Mozart; it is about to get epic in here.

THE ANATOMY OF SPIRITUAL DRESSING

There is energy to the things that you touch, wear, and layer on your body. Think of every step and every layer of your clothing and accessories as an expansion of your energy, ideals, and vibe. When you start digging deeper than the garment itself, you will find that it is less about where something is from and more about what you put with it. Layers in clothes, much like emotional layers, are sexy, so take your time with textures when you dress. You are a walking ball of creative textural energy!

THE MIDDLE   It takes time to finish a full pizza, just as it does to make cardboard look like arm cuffs. So go slow, cut the toilet paper roll in half vertically, and cover the outside in long strips of ribbon. Then fire up the glue gun and begin encrusting the cardboard with rhinestones, costume jewelry, or whatever you can get your hands on, but also think of your materials. Since the base of this cuff is cardboard, and it will be fairly lightweight, use lighter materials to encrust it. This encrustment can go on forever. Just enjoy gluing it on. More is more.

THE END   You have covered two toilet paper rolls in ribbons and encrusted each of them differently. Now you can tie the long dangling ribbon pieces on either side of the cuff around each wrist. You feel like Wonder Woman! Give one of your wrist cuffs to your neighbor downstairs. You even made her a huge thank-you card out of the top of the pizza box. Damn, you're good.

CANVAS TO CLUTCH!

Nothing looks quite as elegant to me as a lady clutch. I have purchased them and sewn them myself, and let me tell you that making them is so much better! Why? Because you can make them oversized and paint them any color you want so you don't have to go searching for the perfect shade! Once you make something so customized for your carrying needs, you will never go shopping again. This project reminds me of my white walking shorts. When I was four and attentively watched my mother sew three Halloween costumes for my sisters and me, I realized she could be my personal seamstress. At this time in my life, I had already figured out that white went with everything and walking shorts had pockets and were a little longer than most shorts. I begged my mother to make WHITE WALKING SHORTS for me and when she did, I never took them off. Wore them every day. They were my four-year-old wardrobe staple that had to fall apart for me to wear something else and this clutch is my 35-year-old staple now. It radiates the same feeling for me with its white canvas crispness, but the ability to paint it and make it mine takes this project to the next level. You do not need your mother to sew this for you as this project is so simple you will make a few of them to go with all your lady outfits.

LEVEL ◆◆

NOTE
If you want to make a naked, white canvas clutch then do not use primed painting canvas. Instead, opt for a heavy-duty unprimed canvas that you can find at the art supply store.

THE LINE-UP
- Any kind of canvas (primed or otherwise)
- A sewing machine or hot glue gun, or both
- Sewing needles & thread
- Double-sided Velcro
- Drop cloth
- Acrylic paint in the colors of your choice
- Paintbrushes

THE BEGINNING

If you've checked the forecast and see that this coming weekend it's going to be raining glitter and sequins outside, run out to the art supply store and buy some supplies. Head home and set up camp. Open the window and let the cool breeze blow in while you sweat over how big to sew this clutch. This is a simple sew, so thread the machine, put your foot on the pedal, and get this canvas clutch rolling.

THE MIDDLE

Cut one big piece of primed canvas about 24 inches in length and 12 inches in width, or whatever size works for you. Place the canvas, primed side up, on a table and then fold the bottom to the top. Now the primed canvas side is on the inside. If you're sewing this clutch, just close up the two side edges. Then fold down the top seams of your clutch so that the edges look finished. All you have to do now is place the self-adhesive Velcro across the top of it for a secure closure!

THE END Once your clutch is assembled, turn your sewing station into a painting one and put the clutch on a drop cloth. Splash paint on the clutch in random designs, or choose a pattern instead. As you dream up new patterns, you might be having visions of a painted clutch store. You are going into business for yourself now because this clutch looks so damn good. You have signed the lease in your head to this small boutique for you to sell your creations. Canvas to clutch has turned into dream come true.

CUT IT UP!

<1HR

I like to cut my clothes. Straight up. No planning, measuring, or sewing. If I want something shorter—with a slit or a different neckline—I just get out my fabric shears and go to it. I realize that this practice is not for everyone, but I get some major compliments on my layering skills and part of this look requires a good proportional cutting job. With this tip in mind, if you find a piece of cheap, cotton clothing and possibly something that you would wear a lot, I recommend that you buy multiples. Let me tell you a story: I was in love with a pair of jeans that I cut. They were perfect in every way: cheap, soft, and oversized. They were frayed to perfection, and even after I washed them, the cuts that I made only got better. I took these jeans on a trip to Punta Cana. And there they stayed. On the way home, these jeans were put in my carry-all that got left behind in the taxi to the airport. I was *devastada*. I lost my pants in the Punta! And I did not snag a backup, so when I got home I did not have another pair to soften the loss. Mistake. Moral of the story: Cut your clothes because it makes them better. But don't take beloved clothing on trips unless you have a backup. **LEVEL** ◆◇◇

THE BEGINNING   Baby, it's cold outside. You have to layer up your long-sleeved cotton shirt with a sweater on top, but you don't want to end up looking bulky. What to do? Cut the ribbed band off the bottom of your sweater so that it's shorter. This means that you can see the cotton top underneath the sweater, and it becomes little less figure-hugging and more comfortable.

THE MIDDLE Fully commit by getting rid of the cuffs from the sweater's sleeves, too. You've done the damage now, so cut the collar to make a deep neckline as well. All of a sudden, you have the hang of it.

THE END The moment of truth happens when you put the sweater back on. You look so cool! It looks like one of those sweaters that you could have purchased at a high-end hippie store, and now you're hooked. This cutting clothes thing is liberating. The last thing you would have ever expected to do is now the first thing you will turn to when you want to step up your layer game. You proceed to spend the remainder of your evening thinking of ways you can cut items in your and your sister's closet. Piles of T-shirts, old jeans, and light cotton sweaters all make the cut! HAPPY CUTTING!

THINGS THAT SHIFTED INSIDE OF ME ARE:

BEAUTY
ON DUTY

I have always been fascinated by the world of beauty. I imagine this is because beauty products are yet another vehicle for artful expression. I have dabbled in being a makeup artist, I spend way too much time at my salon (obviously!), and I live to try new bath products, nail polish adornments, and wild lip colors, like most ladies do. The notion of transforming and enhancing myself with potions and lotions is enchanting to me. I always take things to the next level and that level always leads to me thinking, "What can I make?"

When I was younger, I never considered making my own cosmetics, but I wish I had. Had this notion occurred to me, I would have started wearing makeup at the age of 10. The smell of a L'Oréal lipstick still takes me back to the first tube I ever had. It was light café frosted brown. It was the 90s. Those colors were hot, and so were body oils and those classic "all-in-one" products. This was a simpler and more inspirational time in beauty for me and I remember it fondly. Beyond lipstick, I remember spending my childhood honing my signature smell and styling my hair. While other girls were playing with dolls, I was trying to master hot rollers.

Anyone who knows me knows that I take a shower every morning and a shower or bath at night. This isn't just about being a clean-freak— these dunks in water cleanse me and take me back to a blank canvas. By morning, I am free from the mess of yesterday and ready for painting and transforming. However, finding the right beauty products to do all of this in the saturated beauty market is tough. Choice is everywhere and ingredient lists can become too lengthy or cryptic to understand. I choose to use things from the grocery store or the health food store if I can. If I can't get them there, my beauty regime will become too complicated and less natural.

In this chapter, I challenge you to think about your beauty routine like you think about decorating your space, dressing your body, or working on a craft. Think outside the drugstore and delight yourself with possibility. Consider using what you have and only sourcing from quality and natural sources. This is not to say that I do not love myself some luxury beauty products—I do. But I appreciate a splurge even more when I use up what I have and make the rest.

Beauty is only skin-deep, so let's glitter on the inside!

1+ HR

CLEAN SLATE SALT BATH

If there is one thing I can do, it is draw a mean salt bath! I am like Glinda the Good Witch and my bath is my cauldron where I envision that I am making some healing potion for my body. Think of bath time as a time to release, disconnect, and let go—if only for 15 minutes. I hope you will take on bath time as a form of personal therapy. Set out the ingredients in your bathroom like a ceremonial offering that you must perform to take you to Pleasure Town all the time. PROMISE?

LEVEL ◆◆◆

THE LINE-UP

- Epsom salts
- Pink Himalayan salt
- Baking soda
- Ylang-ylang oil
- Lavender oil
- Sesame oil
- Rose petals
- Cold compress

THE BEGINNING Make sure your bathtub is scoured and cleaned and you have a fluffy towel to jump into afterward. Get that water rolling at the warmest temperature you can stand. Then pour 1 cup of Epsom salts, ½ cup of pink Himalayan salt, and 2 tablespoons of baking soda into the water. Add 6 drops of ylang-ylang and 6 drops of lavender oil. Then put in ¼ cup of sesame oil and sprinkle the rose petals on top. Once the bath is full you will be in a dream state, smelling the goods from the bathroom. Before you hop in, grab a cold compress and keep it accessible.

THE MIDDLE You are luxuriating in the tub. Nothing but the sweet silence of soaking is happening now, so enjoy it. Soak. Soak. Soak. If you like, put your cool compress on the back of your neck so you can stay in a touch longer. If you're anything like me, you'll want to jump out after about 10 minutes because you're getting too hot, but the compress will help keep you in the salted goodness for just enough time to let the cleansing effect take over.

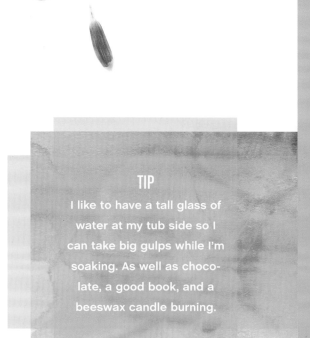

TIP
I like to have a tall glass of water at my tub side so I can take big gulps while I'm soaking. As well as chocolate, a good book, and a beeswax candle burning.

THE END Jump out of the tub and shower off the salt, but don't soap off the oil. Then towel yourself dry, take a huge drink of water, and slip into some clothes that transport you to the coziest place. If you can get into bed after bath time, that would be a dream as this will be when your body is most relaxed! Trust me — you'll sleep like a baby with a calm body and mind.

‹1HR

NAIL POLISH MIX-UP

When I was in fifth grade I started reading *Vogue* magazine cover to cover, and one month, I read that *Vogue* was pairing up with Chanel to hold a contest for a new Chanel nail color. The winner would get the polish made en masse, a trip to NYC, and a $1,000 shopping spree. I entered. I staged a fashion shoot in my back yard, wearing my mother's hunter green faux fur. I took the fake hands that we kept in the TV room to hold our remote controls and mounted my photo in them. Then I painstakingly painted a full set of my mother's fake press-on nails and glued each one to the hands. My color was called Moon Stone Marsh. It was khaki green with silver running through it, but it had a matte finish. In the 90s this had never been seen or worn before. I thought I had a winner. Apparently, I was too ahead of my time. Some chick put glitter in black polish and won. I was not upset. Now, if I'm in the mood for a mani, I mix colors, sprinkle glitter on the wet polish, and treat my nails like a little painting.

LEVEL ◆ ◇ ◇

THE BEGINNING You have somewhere you need to be and realize your manicure leaves something to be desired. But you never fear an unlacquered nail or a chip in the polish, because you are a mixologist! Find a color that makes you happy and paint it in just a few places on your nails, then find another color and fill in the blanks. You can just keep going like this until all your nails are covered in the most confetti-kissed way.

THE MIDDLE If you want to kick it up even more, you know what I'm about to suggest. Get some glitter and sprinkle it overtop of your wet nails. Let it dry, and then marvel at your sparkle. A bonus here is that if you put glitter on your wet nails, it really speeds up the drying process. Believe me—I know!

THE END You can apply a clear coat of polish on top of the glitter so that it stays put, but it's not essential.

IDEA

If you want your nail color to be more customized, pour little bits of certain colors into a little plastic container and mix 'em up. Making your own custom shade is the business! This is also a great option if you don't want to speckle your nails.

HAIR POWDER FOR DAYS

<1HR

I have a confession to make: My hair color is not natural. I know, I know, you thought that this orange tangerine rainbow was all mine because it looks like it grows from my head naturally, but it does not. And, as anyone who has highly processed or dry hair knows, this mane does not like to be washed. You may not have candy-colored hair, but there is a good chance that you wash your hair too often. Yep, you probably do. I like to go a minimum of a week before washing my lady locks, and if I can push it further than that, I will. This little DIY is about supporting the dirty birdies who need to embrace hair oils and increase volume! Most companies that make hair powder don't make it to last in the hair past a day, so you have to powder over and over. They also do not make them in custom colors to match the likes of my mane. So, I have developed my own hair powder recipe. It doesn't matter what your hair color is, you can make a powder to match or enhance it. Let me show you how. LEVEL ◆◆◆

THE LINE-UP

• Pretty container to hold your hair powder
• A mortar and pestle
• 1 cup of cornstarch
• 2 heaping tablespoons of baking soda
• 1 tablespoon of ground cinnamon
• A stick of chalk in the color of your choice (I use orange or pink)
• A hair dryer

THE BEGINNING

Get mixing. Dump the cornstarch, baking soda, and cinnamon into your pretty container. Then, grab one stick of colored chalk in a color that matches your hair and mash it up in the mortar and pestle until it has completely turned to powder. Add it to the container.

THE MIDDLE Your magic powder is ready for the big puff application, so dip your fingers in the mixture and then rub them into your roots all over your head. Do three or four rounds of this until you feel like you have really conquered all of your head, but try not to overdo it. This might be the only time I say that less is more.

THE END Take a hair dryer and dry your hair until the powder and your hair settle into one big volume-enhanced dream. My hair powder lasts for days and keeps the hair looking bouncy and fresh—and with that light hint of cinnamon in the mixture, you'll smell like a cinnamon bun delight!

"It's terrible. She has beautiful eyes and her hair smells like cinnamon!"

RON BURGUNDY

SKIN POTION #9

I have a reputation for the way I smell, and it started when I was a child of the 90s with an obsession with a signature fragrance. I used to collect fragrances mostly because I loved the look and the shape of the bottles they came in. But over the years, the *This Can Be Beautiful* lifestyle has taught me that it's not about how something looks or how pretty the packaging can be. I care more about how something can make me feel and if it's authentically me. When it comes to the body and skin, keeping things natural is a far greater necessity than a pretty bottle on the shelf. I can create pretty bottles with pretty packaging any day of the week; it's much harder to find the right ingredients to make my nose and skin happy. Let me inspire you to say yes to using body oil and to making your own scents that make more sense and smell just like YOU! **LEVEL** ◆◆◇

THE LINE-UP

• Avocado oil or sesame seed oil
• Rose, patchouli, sandalwood, and ylang-ylang essential oils (or any essential oil that smells like a dream to you!)
• An empty glass container or jar to mix and store it in

THE BEGINNING

You're fresh out of the shower and your skin needs a drink of something nourishing and natural, but all you have is some drugstore brand of lotion that's almost gone. Grab the avocado or sesame seed oil from the kitchen and the new essential oils you bought from the health food store, then throw on your robe and start your alchemy!

THE MIDDLE   Find a glass and fill it a quarter of the way to the top with the avocado or sesame oil, or a combination of the two. Then add 6 drops of patchouli oil, 4 drops of rose, 4 drops of ylang-ylang, and 4 drops of sandalwood. Lightly swirl it and let it sit until you have laid out your outfit on your bed and put your makeup on. The longer you let this mixture sit, the better it will smell, as the oils need to settle with each other. If you want the smell to be a little stronger, add more essential oil only one drop at a time, otherwise you risk the mixture becoming a bit too pungent.

THE END   Rub this essential oil dream all over your skin! It only takes a little bit, as a little goes a long way here. And also remember that body oils are not for every outfit. Stay away from using the oil on the days that you are wearing silks or anything that will absorb the oil and stain. Stick with cottons. This will keep for 6 months, or longer in the fridge.

SODA CAN ROLLER DELIGHT

1+ HR

I cannot tell you enough how much respect I have for hot rollers! They are the quickest, simplest, and most magical way to transform your hair and look good in a flash. When I was tiny, I watched my mother set her hair in hot rollers all the time. By the time she was done her makeup, the curlers came out and TA-DA! She was ready and she looked like she'd spent a really long time on her hair! My rainbow locks are often complimented, and I always tell anyone who will listen that hot rollers save the day every time! For those of us who do not always want the hot-rolled curly look, I opt for something that's light and quick, and leaves my hair full of life and volume. If you take a few minutes and down a six-pack of soda pop, you can have a free round of rollers ready for the setting! LEVEL ◆◆

THE LINE-UP

- 6–10 empty soda cans
- Long hair clips
- Can opener
- Hair dryer
- Pale pink spray paint (optional)

WATCH OUT

If your can opener is on the older side, you want to make sure that you sand down or stay clear of any sharp edges once you've taken the lids off the cans so you can roll with ease!

THE BEGINNING Drink as many soda pops as you can so that you can set your hair for cheap! Alternatively, if you want to go rifling through your neighbors' recycling bins, I encourage this behavior instead of drinking soda pop. Either way, go get those cans, girl! After you've collected 6–10 cans, get a can opener and cut the tops off each one, wash them with hot water, and dry them ASAP. Once they're dry, you can spray-paint them pale pink so that they look like those old-school spongy rollers. This step is optional, but you might as well really go for it and make the rollers look pretty. It doesn't work any better or worse if they're pink, I just think they look cuter this way.

NOTE

This styling trick does not work for those who have really tight curly hair. It's for those with hair that is straight or wavy!

THE MIDDLE Put a little of my hair powder recipe (see tip below) on your roots and then run the hair dryer over your hair before you roll it. Once the powder has been blown into the hair, brush your hair out until it's smooth, then section your hair and begin wrapping it around the cans. Secure them by putting a long hair clip into the open end of the can and across the hair. You do this until you have done your entire head. Once you have your pop cans in, blow-dry them one at a time to get the aluminum heated up to set the hair. This should take about 5 minutes. Then take a break and start your makeup.

THE END Your makeup is on, your outfit is picked out, and now all you have to do is get dressed . . . But wait! If you've forgotten about your rollers, no worries! Just mist a little hairspray on your hair and then ROLL outta the house. A real hair pro takes the rollers out just before she walks into a room, and she then shakes it out and owns it. Throw these cans in a bag in your passenger seat and no one will be any the wiser. Bombshell hair!

TIP

This styling tool works in tandem with my hair powder recipe (page 70). If you throw a little hair powder on your dirty dry hair, then blow-dry it with the cans pinned in, it will look amazing and full of volume once you're done!

SUPER POWER SCRUB

One year around Christmas, I was at my favorite grocery store in Toronto's Little India neighborhood and I saw a sale on sugar and olive oil. I continued to walk the aisles of this fragrant grocer until I had thought of a good reason to buy an ungodly amount of sugar and olive oil. Not being much of a cook, a body scrub was the only thing I could think of. I made 60 jars of a body scrub called Get Out of Your Head + Put This on Your Body Scrub. The only thing that I forgot in the recipe was glitter, which I will remedy here, because no shower experience is complete without some fine glitter that dusts your skin with a glimmer without clogging your drain. This is not the thick plastic kind of glitter that will have your landlord visiting till 11:00 pm to snake the pipes. I tried that kind already. It doesn't work as well. LEVEL ◆◆◇

THE LINE-UP

- Vanilla-flavored coffee beans
- Cardamom pods
- Whole cloves
- 1 cup of salt
- 1 cup of sugar
- Olive oil
- Coffee grinder
- Little glass jars
- Micro-fiber very fine glitter
- Scrap fabric
- Ribbons

THE BEGINNING Pull the coffee beans, spices, salt, sugar, and olive oil out of your cupboard—1 cup each of sugar and salt is a good start, but you may need more depending on how many jars of scrub you want to make. Then grab your coffee grinder and get a handful each of the cardamom and cloves all ground up. Grind up a handful of the coffee, and throw it all in a big mixing bowl with the salt and sugar. This is a fragrant experience unlike any other, and if your eyes are closed, you could be in some faraway market or souk.

NOTE

I use coffee because it has caffeine in it. The only time my body needs coffee is during my lame attempts to combat my cellulite. I dream these ground coffee beans will take it away.

THE MIDDLE Blend the mixture with your hands to feel the textures and ingredients and to make sure that everything is soft, scrubby, and fully combined. Check to see if you want more of any of the granules or smells before you put a handful of this magic mixture in a jar. Once you've lightly packed half of the jar with the dry ingredients, fill the rest of it up with olive oil, then add the cherry on top: the dusting of glitter. Take a teaspoon of ultra-fine glitter and watch it coat the top of the oil. Now put a lid on it and seal it up for the using or the giving.

THE END If you're using this scrub for yourself, just place that magical container in the shower. But if you're gifting it, then a little more dazzling is in order! This SUPER SCRUB needs some super fabric scraps to cover the lid to make it special. Cut the fabric to a little bigger than the lid. Drape the fabric over and then tie it down with some ribbon. Write a little lady love note stating the ingredients and your intention for its use, and seal it with love. This will keep for about 6 months.

TRUTH

A real maker cannot take or leave their hands off anything. We don't know how. We need to touch things to know them and get our hands messy to understand them. This does not stop with our makeup or beauty routines, so dive in and use your hands whenever you can, because it makes things feel and apply better.

I FEEL MORE

BEAUTIFUL

BECAUSE:

LOVE
GESTURES

It's not just the big yearly celebrations that matter. To me, the small, non-occasional moments to offer someone a love gesture mean the most. If a "just thinking about you" gesture comes from the heart, it's really the best gift. If you're like me and happen upon little nuggets of goodness throughout the year or make them all the time, think in multiples and stash them away. Additionally, try to think of things that the people in your life will actually use. These are the things that I think about when I see, find, or make a love gesture: Keep it small, fun, useful, or inspiring.

The only thing more important than the love gesture itself is how it is gift-wrapped. And let me tell you, everything you need to create epic wrapping is right at your fingertips. Wrapping a gift is another sign of love. If wrapping has handmade items or glued curiosities all over it, this gift will look unlike anything else — and that is what makes it personal, special, and one-of-a-kind. Think

of interesting, beautiful, and strange ways that you can wrap or give your gifts. It will become your thing! You'll have friends waiting for the next occasion to see what you do. For me, this reputation keeps me on my gift-making toes and pushes me to think outside the gift box when a moment or special occasion comes around.

Sending love notes for no reason is another way to make and spread love gestures. Putting these gratitude messages out into the world is a good practice and sends acknowledgment and care like nothing else can. Love notes can be made from scrap paper, painted onto a strange object, or made from a piece of bark. They take no time and can mean the whole world to the person who receives your magic words. In this chapter, I will inspire you to transform the average things that you have in your home into little treasures that you can give to someone special.

Making something is the gift that keeps on giving!

CEREAL BOX TREASURE

I ate a lot of cereal when I was younger. While other kids were begging for the sugary, fruity stuff, I liked my plain and simple options. The thing about cereal that was always cool was the size of the box and the gifts inside. Not only did I get an XXL amount of my puffed rice delight and a free gift, but I had this huge cardboard container to play with afterward. There is really no end to the goodness that comes from an empty box for me. Even now I stockpile empty boxes, knowing that I will have a purpose for them. So stop buying gift-wrap boxes and bags with the matching tissue. There is a new sheriff in Gift-Wrap Town and his name is Constable Cereal. LEVEL ◆ ◆ ◇

THE LINE-UP

- Box of cereal
- Acrylic paints
- Paintbrushes
- Ribbon
- Yarn
- Newspaper
- Paper tape
- Miscellaneous objects from around the house
- A gift to wrap!

THE BEGINNING Stop digging in the bottom of the cereal bag looking for the temporary tattoo and just pull the whole bag of cereal out and stash it somewhere safe so it won't spill out. Now you have the perfect-sized box to wrap the scarf you knitted for your grandma. Grab your acrylic paints and brushes and start with a nice thick layer of white paint. You'll want to completely cover the entire box with a solid white layer. Once this dries, start to paint some pretty designs all over it. While these designs are drying on the box, start searching the house for things you can make a bow with.

THE MIDDLE Once the paint is dry, get Grandma's scarf inside this box so you can really finish your masterpiece on the outside. To do this, grab some newspaper and paper tape to wrap the scarf, then place it in the box and close it up. Head to the craft cupboard and take your ribbon and yarn and start wrapping it all around the box, layering many ribbons to create a crazy bow. This might be the craziest bow you have ever made, but Grandma likes crazy!

THE END Only Grandma will know it was a cereal box from the sneaky side opening of the gift. The only person who will have more fun than you with this gift is Grandma as she tries to figure out how to unwrap it all. GO, GRANDMA!

DON'T FORGET

Making quick and easy cards is fun. They don't need to be fancy, but they do need to be written with love. I like to use paint chips that I collect from the hardware store to add a little color to my gifts!

GETTING STUCK

Don't think of simple clear tape as your go-to adhesive for wrapping gifts and gestures, because that is so boring. I think that colored tapes, glues, and hot glue all do a "next-level" job of creating standalone design concepts on your parcels.

 # CRACKER CURIOSITY

Having the name Tiffany can be a good thing. It implies high-end diamonds, but also pink spandex and body glitter. It's an interesting dichotomy, which is totally in line with my aesthetic. But the one thing that I definitely do not dig about my name is my initials: TP. To some, TP means "toilet paper." I was always teased about this in school and it has always bothered me! But I am going to reclaim the TP here and now. I have created a craft to make toilet paper and paper towel rolls coveted, cool, and desirable. Stick it, elementary school bullies. LEVEL ◆◇◇

THE LINE-UP

- Toilet paper rolls
- Paper towel rolls
- Saltwater taffy
- Any leftover tissue paper
- Clear cellophane wrapping
- String
- Pom poms
- Ribbons
- Wrapping paper
- Scissors

THE BEGINNING All that water in your diet has you using up TP like crazy! But it's an upside for your crafting repertoire and the perfect excuse to wrap up the gifts you made for your co-workers. Grab all your supplies from the recycling bins and your craft cupboard, and head out to the store for some saltwater taffy or other sweet treat.

IDEA

You can use these paper towel and toilet paper rolls as a wrapping technique for anything small. They can be like a Christmas cracker with lots of trinkets inside, so try filling your tube with more than just your small love gesture! Candy, confetti, glitter, or underwear all make great fillers for these little tubes of love.

THE MIDDLE Fill up the toilet paper and paper towel rolls with the taffy. Then grab some of your old tissue paper and roll it over the toilet paper rolls like a bonbon. Now that your tube is wrapped in tissue, take the clear cellophane wrap and wrap it around the tube in the same fashion as the tissue, tie off the ends with some string, and add a pom pom. Use ribbon too—mix it up!

THE END This wrapping takes no time and it doesn't matter what color combination of tissue paper you use—they all look epic. Your co-workers are going to pee their pants when they see this presentation of your gift-wrapping genius! More TP rolls for you!

DIY POM POM ON THE FLY

Lay a 12-inch piece of yarn down. Then cut additional pieces of yarn to whatever size you want the pom pom; I like them to run about 3 inches long. Take a small pile of yarn and place it in the middle of the long string. Then tie the string around the little pile of yarn, all facing the same direction. REPEAT. Do this until you have the desired puffiness of pom pom. EASY!

CARDBOARD CARDS

<1 HR

I am a summer baby. When I was about to enter ninth grade, my mom asked me what I wanted for my birthday. All I wanted were business cards. Yep, at this point in my life I was convinced that I would be so busy and popular going into high school that I'd need business cards because I'd have no time to write down my name and number on a piece of paper. And that was all they were: white cards with my name and home number written on them in gold. Because of these cards, I had a bit of a reputation during my first year in high school, and let's just say that when the stack of 500 cards was depleted, I was kind of relieved. And speaking of cards, I love making them and I think the homemade ones are the shit. But I don't think that they need to take you a ton of time. Use any cardboard you can find and make little mini paintings on them. It's the recycler's one-of-a kind way to give cards in pure style! LEVEL ◆

THE BEGINNING A big box has arrived filled with all the books that you purchased on a late-night online shopping spree, and now you have all the cardboard you will need to make a bunch of handmade painted cards. Pull out your straight-edge blade right away and start slicing. It doesn't matter if these shapes are perfect rectangles with straight edges. You're just having fun cutting shapes. Cards can come in any shape. Who makes the rules? You make the rules!

SIDE NOTE
It's a good idea to cut these cards in shapes big and small. Sometimes you'll need really small cards and sometimes you'll need really big ones, so give yourself some variety.

THE MIDDLE You have all your card shapes cut out and now you're ready to paint. You'll only be painting the one side, so don't pour out a huge amount of paint. Lay out the newsprint, spread the cards over the table top, pour out your paints, fill a cup with water, and get those brushes rolling! Some cards are abstract, others have messages written on them, and others just have hearts!

THE END Your painted cards are all done and dried, and now you want to add some kind of metallic flair to make them pop. Pull out your gold leaf kit, or if you don't have one, pull out the white glue and aluminum foil; both give beautiful results. The technique is much the same for both, but the gold leaf is a little thinner and more delicate to work with. Refer to the instructions in your gold leaf kit.

FYI
Keep a stash of gold or silver pens, white or pastel-colored pencil crayons, or a white gel pen on-hand for these cards. When you're writing on cardboard you'll need a color that will pop against the brown.

HANDMADE HOSTESS

<1HR

THE LINE-UP

- Rose pastilles
- Honey
- Chocolate
- Fancy underwear
- Cereal box treasure (optional)

IDEA

It's always a good idea to have a little stash of things set aside for giving. Even if you think they're little things, they're good to have stockpiled in case you need something on the fly.

I never like to show up to someone's house without a little toast to the host. It's such a lovely and kind thing to be invited to someone's home for a little DO, and showing up empty handed is a DON'T. I always bring things I think are wonderful. Useful, funny, delicious, pretty, or "I would never buy that for myself" kind of items are the perfect picks. One of my most celebrated and common hostess gifts is an economy-sized pack of toilet paper. Everyone needs toilet paper and everyone loves to show up to someone's house with something monstrously huge in her hands. I have never had a complaint about this gift and it always puts a smile on my host's face. Plus, I always put a beautiful big bow on it, which makes the gift even funnier. But if you do not want to express your gratitude by way of toilet paper, here is a concept sure to dazzle the host with a little local support on top! LEVEL ◆ ◆ ◆

THE BEGINNING You've found a local crafter who makes the most outstanding high-waisted underwear out of up-cycled cashmere sweaters! You want to support your pal, so you buy yourself a pair and then decide you should have a few pairs tucked inside of your hostess drawer for when you get an invite to the next lady dinner. None of your gal pals would ever buy these for themselves, but you know they would love them!

THE MIDDLE When you get home you find an email from your bestie saying that she's hosting a cocktail party at her place for a load of ladies to raise some money for charity. You immediately run to your hostess drawer to see what you have to bring. You find rose pastilles, imported chocolate, raw honey, and now these amazing undies! All of them would do! What to choose?! Check back on my cereal gift box idea on page 84 and start packaging up these little gems.

KEEP IT SIMPLE

The easiest gift is something that looks great on its own, so look for something that has lovely packaging and all you'll have to do is frost it with a tassel or pom pom on top!

THE END Tonight is the big night and you're off to the cocktail party. For a final touch, make some pom poms to go on your gift (see page 87) or a pink bubble wrap bow (see page 96). You don't need to give multiple things to your hostess. One item with a beautiful decorative tag and tassel is a beautiful gesture of love!

PAPER BAG PRIESTESS

I have a thing for craft paper. I always have, and I always will—the crafter in me is romanced by it. When I was designing the website for my art studio many years ago, the background for the site was brown craft paper. All of my crafting tables were lined with brown paper and I always sent home art in brown paper bags. There's a cool juxtaposition between very bold colors, glitter, and the natural look of craft paper. This juxtaposition has stayed with me always, and whenever I wrap something—a table, a present, or a parcel to be shipped—I think of how I can throw texture in the mix and I always reach for the craft paper. This little wrapping inspo will have you running home from the grocery store and wrapping your next love gesture with ease and excitement using only your brown grocery bags and some leftover crafting scraps. **LEVEL** ◆ ◇ ◇

THE LINE-UP

- **Brown paper bags**
- **Stapler**
- **Hot glue gun**
- **Leftover trims, lace, or ribbons**
- **Markers**
- **Scissors**

THE BEGINNING You made a T-shirt for your sister. You want to wrap it in a way that will delight her and throw her off. And you happen to have a surplus of brown paper bags from the grocery store. Cut off the top and bottom of the bag, then place the T-shirt inside and staple all around the edges.

FYI

You can cut the brown paper bags into any shapes that you like. I personally like a heart or round shape, but it depends on what you're wrapping, so cut your shape accordingly.

THE MIDDLE Now that the T-shirt is trapped under a layer of brown craft paper bag, pull out the hot glue gun and all of your leftover scrap trims. Start to glue them, one by one, all the way around the bag, starting from the outside edge. You're creating a layered, textured effect. Keep laying the trim on top of the glue and working your craft scraps into the middle of the bag, until you have a nice space to write a message.

THE END Now that you have your textured trims glued down, write a love message for your beloved sister. Short, sweet, and to the point. Then drop this love morsel off ASAP so she can proudly wear her new T-shirt as soon as possible. She might just love the trim-adorned wrapping job so much that she steals the idea when she goes to wrap her next gift!

PINK BUBBLE BOWS

<1HR

Some loves last forever, and it appears my love for the color pink is one of them. It doesn't matter what the product is—if it comes in the color pink, I will love it, use it, collect it, and want it near me until the end of time. Even when I was small, I would make my sisters settle for an alternative color. They would get green, yellow, orange, or blue, and I always got pink. Currently, I am really into things that should not be pink but are, like bubble wrap. I cannot remember the first time I saw pink bubble wrap but it has been a hot love affair ever since. I got the wacky notion to make a bow out of bubble wrap one year for the holidays, because I wanted a big pink bow on my outdoor wreath but didn't want to use a simple ribbon, because it would get ruined by the snow. So, I opted to use something more durable. Ever since, I have made pink bubble wrap bows and they've become one of my signatures. The best part about this idea is that you can use the bubble wrap from items that come to you in the post. **LEVEL** ◆◆

THE LINE-UP
• Bubble wrap (preferably pink)
• Wire of any kind that's easy to use
• Scissors

SPARKLE
You can get some spray glue and dust some glitter on top of this bow if you want a little extra glitz!

THE BEGINNING You just received a shipment of picture frames that you ordered to frame some family photos and they arrived packed in pink bubble wrap! This discovery might be more exciting than the frames themselves. Unwrap the frames and carefully remove the tape from the edges of the bubble wrap so it remains unscathed. Now that your bubble wrap is loose, grab your scissors and some wire and start cutting widths of bubble wrap up to 4 inches wide in whatever length you have.

THE MIDDLE Take your strips of bubble wrap and gather them in bunches, in little bits at a time, making loops and wiring the bottom of the loops together so they start to resemble the loop on a bow. Make about three or four loops/bows. You can make these bows as big or as small as you like; my measurements are only for the basic ones that I've made. If you want to take this craft to the next level, then cut the bubble wrap thinner or wider and see the new proportions that are possible!

THE END It's time to put the tails on the bows. As with most bows, the end pieces dangle down, so cut a few strips of bubble wrap and wire them to your looped-up bundles. TA-DA! You have your bubble wrap bow! It will look like a bubblegum dream atop any love gesture and it will kill in style and recycled charm while not killing your budget or the planet.

FYI

Bubble wrap comes in all kinds of different bubble sizes. It's a good idea to cut the width of each strip when you're making bows in accordance with the size of the bubble. If you have bigger bubbles, you do not want to cut through them—that would burst your bubble and the fun! Follow the size of the bubbles carefully.

I WANT TO MAKE
LOVE LETTERS
AND GIFTS FOR:

ARTY PARTY

I would like to set the record straight off the top. I do not like to cook. This chapter is not about mini sandwiches, fondue recipes, or some custom cocktail that I developed. Rather, this chapter is about helping you make huge occasions less stressful by using things you already have so you don't have to run to the store 500 times. Using the *This Can Be Beautiful* mantra, I will encourage you at every turn to use your leftover party supplies, pull out the good china, use the silver if you have it, and own your love for paper plates and plastic cutlery all at the same time. Because, let's be honest, nobody loves doing dishes all the time. Mix it up! Life is short!

My experience with this started when the hectic nature of event planning came at me like a tidal wave and swept me into a sea of details for many years. I was not properly equipped, I was not wearing a bathing suit, I did not have a surfboard, and I was not wearing SPF and dammit I'm a ginger! When I was asked to design and style one wedding it had a ripple effect. It quickly became 20 weddings, and so, for a portion of my life, this is what I did. I had never thrown events so huge in my life, but all I ever kept thinking was, "Throw the party that you would want to attend." This personal mantra is what got me through the stressful moments and what landed me multiple spreads in wedding magazines and blogs.

I digress.

What I am trying to say is that deep inside of all of us are party planners: We all want to be the people who have friends, neighbors, or family over and are prepared and dazzling. Everyone has their own social circle, style, and way of entertaining. I want you to do this your way. I don't subscribe to a perfectly appointed table that's polished and perfect at all times. When you rock the mindset of *This Can Be Beautiful*, you know that what you have is enough and that with a little time and imagination any occasion can be a hit.

My style of entertaining? Decorate the living crap out of a space and order in the food. That way, no one will judge my lack of cooking because they're distracted by the decorations in the room. I'll have sent out handmade or inventive invitations, and will decorate with wild garlands, fun table settings, and a little loot for my guests to take home. Instead of guests asking what my stellar brownie recipe is, they'll be watching, engrossed, as I host a mini craft class showing my peeps how to make the garland I created. This is all a part of my master plan: *Teach the world to craft*. See, we all have our own agenda.

If there is one takeaway that you will have from this chapter, it's that the "more is more" style of decorating is always the answer behind an epic party. As long as you properly sugar-up your guests and play great music, everyone will have the time of their lives. I promise! So think big: Have treasure hunts! Decorate your space with forts instead of chairs and couches! Bring back loot bags for adults! Empty your cupboards of mix-and-match china and break the rules.

Now, grab your caftan and let's GO!

THE LINE-UP
• Plastic glasses
• White cardstock paper
• Gold pen
• Glitter
• Ribbon or pom poms
• White glue

MESSAGE IN A GLASS

1+ HR

Believe it or not, I am not a drinking woman. These wild and crazy projects might suggest otherwise, but it's true. I come up with my concepts while sober, but I always try to use the beautiful glassware that drinks and cocktails come in for styling vignettes, serving a dessert, or handing out invitations. Handing out invitations might be the strangest use for glassware ever, but I always seem to have leftover plastic glasses or I find some dollar store ones that are perfect for this kind of thing. With a quick drop of a coaster-sized invite into the glass, you're in the invitations business. LEVEL ◆◆

THE BEGINNING You need to have the ladies over for a catch-up because things have been too crazy for everyone to hang lately. You spot some dollar store pink margarita glasses and pick up just enough to have your best gals over for a love-in. Head home and pull out the cardstock, gold pen, glitter, ribbon, and white glue.

THE MIDDLE Trace the top of the glass so you know how big to cut the circle of paper. Then cut as many circles as you have glasses and pull out your gold pen. Write out the details. I suggest something cute like, "I THINK YOU'RE REFRESHING! Come over for some girl time at my place this Friday at 8:00 pm." Then dip the edges of the cup in white glue and rim it promptly in glitter. Let the glass dry.

THE END Once your invites are dry, fill up the glass with some glitter and pop the invites inside. Now make little pom poms or tassels for the stems of the glasses (see page 87). Drop them off in your friends' mailboxes and your Friday night will be filled with delight!

TIP

Write the information that you want on the invites on a separate piece of paper so you know what you're writing and how everything is spelled. Too many times have I blown through paper while handwriting details on the fly and running out 'cause I missed a detail or spelled something wrong. Practice!

GOOD IDEAS

If by chance all of your lady friends are in one spot when you pass the invites out, it would be so cute to put the glasses on a tray for serving. It takes the whole concept to the next level and makes everyone so excited for the party!

FYI

Get into the habit of making something "just because." It's always when we need something at the last minute that we scramble to get it done and succumb to craft stress. Get ahead of the party-planning game and make fun décor to stash away for the next party.

2+ HRS

GARLAND LAND

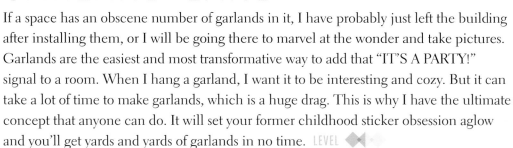

If a space has an obscene number of garlands in it, I have probably just left the building after installing them, or I will be going there to marvel at the wonder and take pictures. Garlands are the easiest and most transformative way to add that "IT'S A PARTY!" signal to a room. When I hang a garland, I want it to be interesting and cozy. But it can take a lot of time to make garlands, which is a huge drag. This is why I have the ultimate concept that anyone can do. It will set your former childhood sticker obsession aglow and you'll get yards and yards of garlands in no time. LEVEL ◢◣ ▸

THE LINE-UP

- **Neon circle stickers**
- **Scissors**
- **String**
- **Tape**

THE BEGINNING You're at an office supply store buying ink cartridges for your printer and you happen to see a bargain bin filled with circular stickers in assorted neon colors. Scoop up as many as you can and store them in your craft cupboard for a rainy day. The next time your family BBQ is canceled due to rain and there's a Meg Ryan rom-com marathon running, pull out your stickers, scissors, and string and start assembling your Garland Land.

THE MIDDLE Tape one end of the string to the side of a table. Unravel some length of string across the width of the table and then tape that end down too. Having the string taped to the table will make it easier to place one sticker behind the string and one on top of it without making a mess. Seal the stickers to each other with the string trapped in the middle, at whatever distance apart you would like. You can place the string anywhere inside the circle for a varied pattern within the garland. You can also fold one sticker in half and seal it to itself. Or even cut shapes out from the stickers, so you vary up the look! If you're crying while you watch *When Harry Met Sally* and you mess up your sticker spacing, it's okay—this garland need not be perfect.

THE END You have used up your stickers, so stash your garland in your craft cupboard. You are ready for any occasion or special event, so when the moment strikes, you'll be ready to cover your space with circular Garland Land dreams.

TIP

If you have the lid of a shoe box or a brown paper shopping bag on-hand, wind your finished garland around it as you make it so it doesn't get tangled.

LOOT JARS

When I was young, I used to plot all summer long about the theme for my birthday parties. I wanted the same heart-themed party until I was six years old, but then I moved into cooler themes like makeup and ballet slippers. And when I'd prepare for my parties, I would obsess over what went inside the loot bags. The makeup-themed loot was the top dog! Everyone got their own lipstick, nail polish, and nail file and a huge chocolate bar. To this day, I can still remember the thrill I had in my little heart passing out those loot bags when the party was over. I was so excited to get and give all my little underage friends their own makeup! Today, the thing that I find underwhelming about loot and swag are the bags that they come in. Being the re-user that I am, I cannot help but think that jars are the way to go. You can see all the goodies inside them and you can always reuse the jar for something else! So let's jar-up the loot from now on, shall we? LEVEL ◆ •

REMEMBER

Just because you're an adult now doesn't mean that you should not create a killer loot jar for your adult friends. Let's stop taking ourselves so seriously and remember the thrill of the loot and the joy it brings.

THE LINE-UP

- Tube of glitter glue
- Tinsel
- Beaded bracelets
- Mini plastic dinosaurs
- Party horns
- Chocolate kisses
- Glass jars
- Scrap fabric
- Pom poms (see page 87)
- Hot pink tags
- Yarn
- Scissors

THE BEGINNING It's canning season and everyone is giving you pickles. Between the cucumbers, the tomatoes, and the sales at the local hardware store on jars, you're stocked up. You have some tinsel left over from Christmas and Easter, and your niece has a birthday coming up! Why not tell your sister that you will handle the loot bags? Get the head count and head to your craft cupboard and dollar store so you're ready to stuff these jars with love.

THE MIDDLE Lay everything out on a table and divide each item according to the quantity you need. Start with the tinsel, add the bracelets, a dinosaur, party horn, and chocolate kisses and make it a stuffing free-for-all. If you find yourself digging into the chocolate kisses, be sure not to put any empty foil wrappers in the jars. When you're done, screw the lids on these sparkling jars of love and start cutting fabric and making pom poms (see page 87).

THE END You've covered the lid of the jar with fabric and made a round of pom poms, so you can tie them onto the lids of the jars and secure the fabric. Your loot jars are ready to roll and your niece is going to have the best birthday in the biz.

GOOD IDEAS

If you aren't throwing the party, it's always a sweet idea to ask the hostess what you can do or bring to help out. It will take some responsibilities off her shoulders and will allow you to inject your party style into the event.

TP STREAMERS

<1 HR

This little decorating idea may remind you of Halloween, but it's not scary. The only thing scary about Halloween for me was that I entrusted my mother to surprise me at lunchtime on October 31 with my costume for that night. It thrilled her, and I didn't really care what I was, as long as it was FUN. In second grade, I came home, ate my peanut butter sandwich, then got decked out in fishnet stockings and armbands, a corset, a black and gold wig, and dark, heavy makeup. I thought I looked cool, but I didn't know what I was supposed to be. So, I asked my mom. Quickly and simply she replied, "A lady of the night." When I went back to school and my classmates asked me what I was, I told them what my mom said, hoping one of them would know what that phrase meant. None of them did . . . except my teacher. She asked me to tell people that I was a punk. Years later I figured out what a lady of the night was and I haven't let my mother live it down. Trust that this craft idea will not be as humiliating as that one was, but it will warrant some comments and questions all the same.

LEVEL ◆ ◆

THE LINE-UP

- 4 rolls of toilet paper
- Food coloring
- 4 bowls
- Water

TIP

The less food coloring you use, the more pastel the color looks on the toilet paper. So, if you're decorating for Halloween, I recommend going for broke and pigmenting that water!

THE BEGINNING   It's the Friday before Halloween, and you've been working like a wild woman on a killer deadline. But you promised your gal pal you would help her set up her fright-night party on Saturday night. Without the time or desire to run to a party supply store, you grab a few rolls of toilet paper from your economy-sized stash and some food coloring and make your own streamers. Dilute 50 drops of any kind of food coloring in a bowl half-filled with water. Then place the toilet paper inside the bowl and let it soak up some of the water. Pull it out, turn it over, and dip the other side of the roll.

THE MIDDLE   This craft takes hardly any time. You can mix a few types of food coloring to get fun new hues from the basic supplied colors, so explore your options and spice it up! Once you've dipped four rolls of toilet paper in different colors, leave them on your patio or in a cool spot for a day to dry.

THE END   Set to work unraveling your DIY streamers all over your gal pal's place on Saturday night. To make it extra Halloween-y, throw some of it on the tree in front her house. The place is festive and nobody knows that it's TP!

FYI

Dyeing the TP is a great way to spice up a "make-your-own-dress-with-toilet–paper" party game. It will take the plain white TP concept to the next level and throw a little Technicolor in the mix.

NAPKIN RING NECKLACE

Every time I see one of those fancy napkin rings, I can't help myself. I slip it on my finger hoping it will fit. But the fancy napkin rings are meant to fit a giant's fingers and aren't something that I can wear. That said, they've gotten me thinking: What if I created a napkin ring adornment that was a take-home piece of jewelry? I love hosting evenings where my guests leave with something that reminds them of the time we shared. This napkin ring necklace idea will make an impact on your table and on your guests. **LEVEL** ◆◆

THE BEGINNING Grab some lengths of ribbon from your craft cupboard and some big wooden beads that you can use for necklaces. Place a few big beads on your ribbon, then one big statement gemstone for the middle, and a few more beads to finish up the other side. If you want to add a few other items to the necklace, go for it! Add your own style and keep it easy. Make sure to make one necklace for each guest.

THE LINE-UP

- Ribbon
- Wooden beads
- Gemstones
- Cloth napkins

FYI

I found these gemstones at the dollar store. Keep your eyes peeled for cheap, cool things you can collect in mutliples.

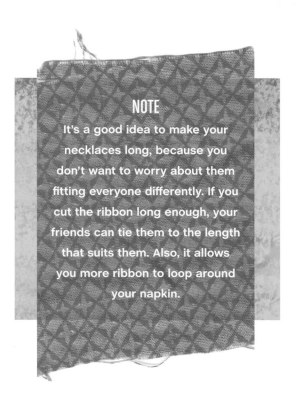

THE MIDDLE Collect some cloth napkins from the kitchen and start to wrap your necklaces around each one. Tie the ribbon of the necklace around the cloth napkin and make a pretty bow! This is super easy and looks extravagant!

THE END Once you've wound your necklaces around the napkin, set the table and call for the Indian takeout. When the food has arrived and your friends have shown up, sit them down immediately and show and tell them how much you love them all with the napkin ring necklaces that they see on their plates. You are such a GEM!

◆ 1+ HR SETTING THE TABLE

I love caftans for all occasions. I often get lectured about my caftan collection because mine are the most unflattering, oversized, and highly patterned clothes most people have ever seen. One of the many reasons that I love caftans is that you instantly look like the 1960s version of the hostess with the mostest, with a side of the *Bewitched* nose wiggle. These unique items of clothing will help you pull off any crazy table setting and make it very clear to anyone attending your party that you are the hostess. The way I dress a table is similar to how I dress my body. I want big, bold, playful, comfortable, and easy things all around me. Food that people will want to grab and eat, and that will taste wonderful and look wonderful, too. I want my tables to look like an experience rather than an appointed collection of standard things. If I can make a Dream Land table setting out of only crazy things I can find in my craft cupboard or at the grocery store, then my stress levels are low and my party energy can be high! Use what you have and mix it up. Don't kill yourself trying to be something that you're not, and try to have more fun than your guests. And if you rock a caftan, you'll be more comfortable than them too! LEVEL ◆◆◆

THE LINE-UP

- Paper plates
- Cups of any kind
- Teacups and saucers
- Plastic cutlery
- Silverware (if you have it)
- Champagne
- Cream and sugar
- Cake
- Macarons
- Chocolate rabbits
- Sugar cookies
- Chocolate coins
- Candy necklaces
- Rocket candy
- Faux butterflies
- Flagging tape
- Faux flowers
- Greenery
- Tissue corsages
- Party crowns
- Sparklers
- Confetti
- Colored streamers
- Colored feathers
- A good caftan

MEMORY LANE

Remember on page 22 when we sprayed a glass punch bowl with spray paint? Well, this is the perfect time for you to put those spraying skills to good use. Look for any sad glassware and spray it up to make your table more interesting.

MIX IT UP

It's important to have lots of napkins and water at a party, so make sure your kitchen is well stocked with both. In addition to the sweets, add a salty contrast just in case. As well, I love putting out little candies and grab bags for people to take and nibble at on the ride home!

THE BEGINNING You've been to the grocery store and collected all of the sweet treats that you'll need for your table. Pull out all of your paper plates and leftover party supplies, and all of your glasses, teacups, and decorative dessert ware. Think about displaying things in different colors, levels, and containers. Start getting the little things together before you make your centerpiece.

THE MIDDLE Once you have all of your nibbles in cool containers, and your teacups and accoutrements are ready to go, you can turn your attention to the centerpiece. If the grocery store flowers are looking a little lackluster, don't despair. Get some green foliage and throw some fake butterflies on it to make a lush setting. Get the cake on the cake tray and lay out the forks, knives, and spoons, and soon you will be ready!

THE END You have your party crown on, your caftan is rocking, and all of the details are set for the party. You have your lighter at the ready for the sparklers, your streamers are in full effect, and you have confetti and colored feathers to throw when the moment grabs you, too. All you need is music, so put on your favorite Swinging Sinatra playlist and your evening is made. Your house is primed with many areas for your friends to chill and you have lots of yummies to offer. A bottle of champagne is there for your bubbly pals and your teacups can be used for both bubbly and tea. Enjoy the party!

PAYING IT FORWARD

I like to give away as much as I can after a party because it gives me less to clean up after everyone is gone. So if there's extra food, candy, flowers, or dessert, make sure to have little "to-go" bags and containers to send it all home with your guests.

THE GUEST LIST
FOR MY NEXT
PARTY IS:

TIFFANY
TRAVELS

Exploring the world can help you add new colors and places to your creative heart where the sky really is the limit. For me, traveling restores my inventiveness and furthers my love of making something from nothing. If you can find the time to see someplace new, go on vacation, or just get away for the weekend, celebrate this opportunity by enhancing your travel gear and creating some beautiful, inexpensive items that will prepare you for your trip! The crafts in this chapter will psych you up before you go, and as a bonus, you'll be able to show the world your style.

I don't start thinking about upcoming trips until the trip is practically upon me, and then I pack and gather like a wild woman. I usually realize about 48 hours before going anywhere that I have to get prepared. This usually leaves me with at least one sleepless night of crafting and preparing, which in turn means I sleep well on the plane. And some of my best outfits are born from packing a bunch of clothes without much thought and finding ways to make the combinations work. Maybe this is all part of the plan. As you know, I try not to overthink any of it!

Some of my travel creations end up on many excursions, so when I want to freshen up my gear, I can replace them in a hot minute, knowing that I haven't invested too much time or money. Same with clothes—I don't bring my all-time favorite pieces on trips, but I do alter clothes to make them "new-ish" before going away. I remember the night I feverishly ripped and aged a pair of boyfriend jeans with a straight-edge blade before a trip to New York. I had it in my head that one of my comfy sweaters would look great with ripped jeans. I did not want to lose my beloved ones, so I quickly made a pair.

As a former flight attendant, I can tell you that the less you travel with, the more memorable your journey becomes. I don't get too attached to the things that I take along. I know that I need items that are comfortable, light, and dripping in my travel style. In my case, it often involves pink and pom poms, because I don't do subtle very well. You can pretty much see my suitcase gliding along on Baggage Claim A all the way from Baggage Claim F!

And that's as it should be, because this chapter is all about making things quintessentially yours, even when you're away from home. I don't believe travel gear needs to be replaced often or even purchased in the first place. With a few items from around the house or the craft cupboard, you can have your own bag tag, passport holders, garment bags, and so much more. So save your monies for the adventures and not for the fancy new luggage that will be stored in a closet later.

Bring what you know you'll need to have a wonderful time and leave the rest to chance.

**Travel light!
The future is bright!**

THE LINE-UP
- Garment bag
- All different sizes of washi tape
- String of sequins
- Hot glue gun

GARMENT BAG SWAG

<1 HR

When I walk through an airport, I like to channel the old days where luggage was a work of art, filled with color, style, and pattern—nothing matched and yet everything made sense. I also like to think about how to easily transport my lady garments so they don't get wrinkled en route to my destination. If my trip is a quick one and I have a handful of garments that I need to maintain, a garment bag is my best friend. Nice stores hand them out for free when you purchase something expensive, or you can buy a cheapie three-pack of plastic garment bags. But these pre-fab renditions all leave something to be desired. In the event that my garment bags are worse for wear upon my return, I do not want to pour too much money or time into them! But with a little hot glue, washi (a Japanese paper tape), and sequins, you can have a garment bag all your own and ensure some head-turning at the airport with people thinking, "Who is that girl?!" And if it makes it back safely from the trip, I reuse it. If not, I can remake it! Fasten your seat belts, friends, and let's take a trip to Adhesive Town! LEVEL ◆◆◆

GOOD IDEAS

These garment bags are practically disposable, so don't go crazy spending loads of time tricking them out. If the garment bag doesn't fare well on the trip, you can decorate another one all over again next time.

FYI

Colored paper tapes can come in a variety of widths. You can get it in traditional tape width or in extra-wide widths. It's worth a little searching at the craft store, as this extra-wide paper tape is the business. If you don't have or don't want to head out for paper tape, use what you have! Colored masking tape, painter's tape, duct tape, or electrical tape are all great backups. They all come in such wonderful and fun colors.

THE BEGINNING You have a trip to New York City looming and you only want to pack dresses. If you fold them up in a suitcase, they'll get wrinkled, so your best bet is to opt for a carry-on garment bag. Search out the plastic garment bag stash that you have in your "just in case" drawer. Then head to the craft cupboard and pull out your colored paper tapes, a string of sequins, and your hot glue gun. It's time to tell the world how stylish you are by way of a garment bag . . .

THE MIDDLE Your first move is to "candy-stripe" this garment bag with the different paper tapes you have on-hand. This decorating only takes a few minutes and will instantly transform your plain white plastic wrapping into a candy-coated bedazzlement. Then you'll want to trim the garment bag with gold sequins (because why not), so fire up the hot glue gun and glitter up the edges. This will finish the bag off so beautifully and really give it that DIY glow.

THE END Once you've stuffed your dresses into the tricked-out candy-striped garment bag, you'll only need a small carry-on for your undergarments and cosmetics. You might wonder why you never traveled so light before—but now you're a cheap bedazzled garment bag devotee for life! You might also find that as you enter the plane, the flight attendant will offer to hang your swag in the front closet (probably because she wants to stare at your crafting styles all flight long). SCORE!

NOTE
If you travel with style, you get treated in style. Make sure to put your best foot forward in an airport. Because travel can be stressful for some, be the person who gives their fellow passengers a smile and some eye candy to enjoy in-flight. The world needs more of that!

COFFEE FILTER FLOURISH

I am not a coffee drinker. If I was, we'd all be in trouble. I am naturally a little "up," but if you were to come to my Glitter Suite, you'd think I made a pot of coffee hourly. I stockpile coffee filters like a paper goods hoarder. I cannot run out of uses for the everyday coffee filter—there is something magical about its ruffled edge and that white, absorbent paper material that makes a crafty gal like me perk right up! You can wrap things in them, you can cluster them and make wall hangings, and you can make little pom poms, too. Here, I make oversized rosettes to adorn the top of my suitcase and help identify my luggage. Once you've done this, you'll be able to spot your luggage from a mile away and those little rosettes will make you happy every time you see your suitcase coming around the carousel at the baggage claim. LEVEL ◆◆◆

THE LINE-UP

- Embroidery thread
- Thick plastic needle with a wide eye
- Nail scissors
- A few packs of white traditional coffee filters
- A tray of watercolor paint
- Paintbrush

THE BEGINNING You're headed on a trip to see your aunt in Arizona who you've not seen in a while. You want to wow her with your crafty skills and styles, so you start by adorning your suitcase with these coffee filter rosettes. And while you're at it, why not make her some as a little gift, too? I'll bet that your kitchen has some filters stored way in the back from when you last used your old coffee maker. Head to the craft cupboard and grab some embroidery thread, a plastic needle (so you can do this craft on the fly—or while you fly), and some nail scissors.

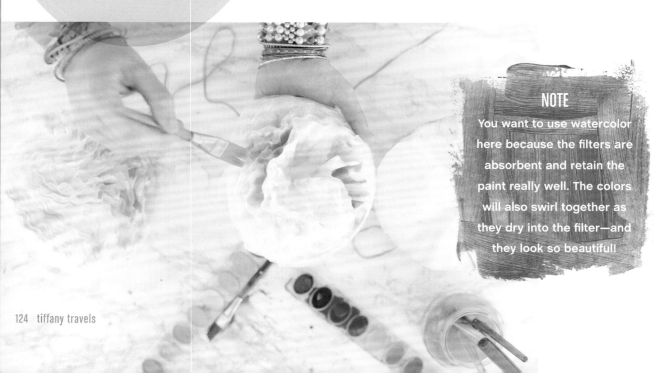

NOTE

You want to use watercolor here because the filters are absorbent and retain the paint really well. The colors will also swirl together as they dry into the filter—and they look so beautiful!

THE MIDDLE Thread the needle so that you have a long piece of embroidery thread and then tie a nice knot at the end. Start to pierce the filters in the middle and add them to the length of embroidery thread, one after the other. Crunch them all up together as you thread them so that they make a nice cluster. Once you have a full bundle, just tie a knot at the back to keep the filters all together. Repeat until you have three coffee filter rosettes for your lady suitcase and a few to give to your aunt!

SPREADING THE LOVE

These filters are inexpensive and easy to make, so if they fall off or go missing in transit, at least you know that you're sprinkling DIY flowers all over the world like a Bollywood movie! When you get home you can make some more.

THE END No doubt you have fallen in love with your white rosettes. But life without color is not the way you roll, so pull out your little tray of watercolors and lightly dust the tops of your rosettes with some much watered-down watercolor and a nice wet brush. Let them dry off, tie them onto your suitcase handle, and you're ready to take to the skies!

BIGGER IS BETTER
The more coffee filters you use the puffier the rosette is!

BAG TAG BLITZ

In the past, I often found myself checking my luggage and filling out one of those sad, paper, airline-logoed bag tags. I needed to sort this bag-tag situation stat! If you're like me, then you realize that the prefabricated bag tags have no pizzazz, so you avoid them—but this is no excuse not to have one! I have one really fancy bag tag that I use on my carry-on, but now the one I use on my checked luggage is an eye-catching delight. When I crafted with kids at my art studio many years ago, I discovered the beauty of trapping confetti in between two pieces of clear moving tape. It takes no time and yields amazing results! I've tweaked this technique to apply these stylish craft ideas in my current life. Using all the leftover confetti that I collect from swag bags, presents, and cards, I can fill one side of tape easily with confetti and the other side with my details! LEVEL ◆◆

THE LINE-UP
- A marker pen
- A piece of cardstock
- Clear packing tape
- Glitter
- Confetti
- Scissors
- String
- A hole punch

THE BEGINNING As a crafter, you likely have gorgeous jars of confetti and glitter that have been a long-growing collection. There's an all-girls getaway coming up and you want to do something special to get everyone excited about the trip, and the cutest idea would be to make everyone their own bag tags! Head to the craft cupboard, grab your fancy marker pen and some cardstock, and write each of your pals' details and addresses on the card stock in a fun way.

THE MIDDLE You have all your pals' deets written out and now you can make the tags. Place two pieces of the clear tape (or as many pieces as you need to cover the cardstock) alongside each other, sticky side up, and place the card details-side-down. Then, sprinkle the whole back half of the card with your swag glitter and confetti concoction, and close it up with two more pieces of clear tape. You'll have a package with your deets on one side, and glitter and confetti on the back.

THE END Trim up the edges so that your bag tags have a nice border of glitter and confetti sticking out, then grab the hole punch and create a little hole at the top to loop in some string. Now get the tags all strung up and ready for the girls' getaway!

GOOD IDEAS
If you don't like the glitter and confetti concept (and how could you not?), then try using magazine clippings, photos that you have, or any type of patterned paper that gets you all a-flutter inside!

Violet V.
169 East 71st
New York, NY
14081

Ginger R.
88 Broadway St.
Toronto, ON
M80 2S1.

Belly Beauty
10 Lovers Lane
New York, NY
14020

Lady Love.
8 Electric Lane.
Toronto, ON.
M6J 2T3.

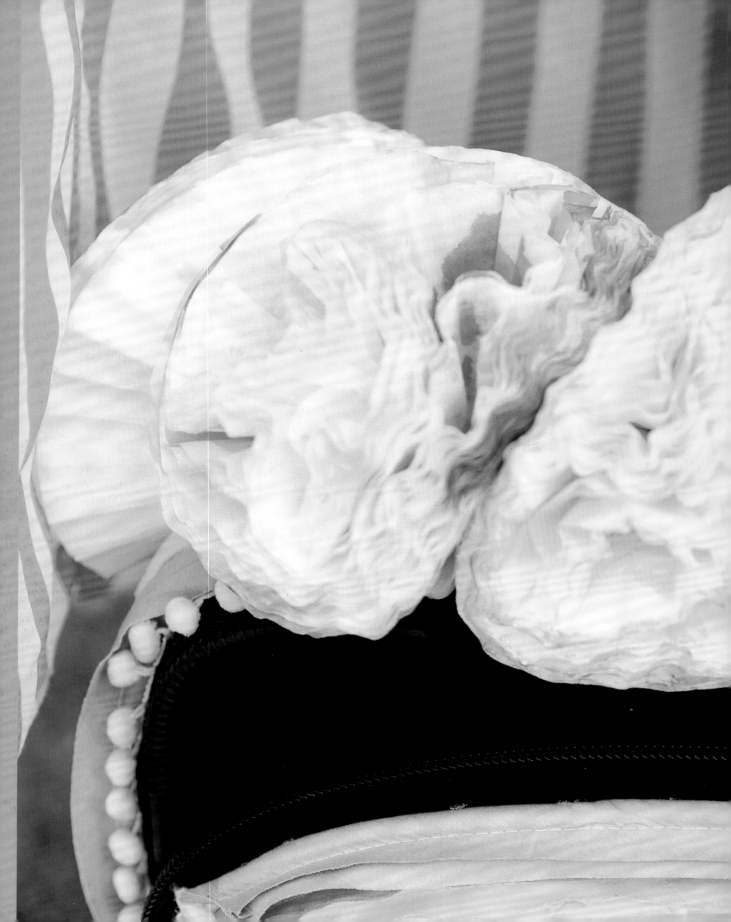

COSMETIC BAG TAPE-UP

<1 HR

FYI
There are so many adorable duct tapes on the market right now in all kinds of different colors. No one will ever know you're concealing a resealable freezer bag once you're done taping it up.

One of my earliest childhood memories is the Christmas I discovered that Santa was my mom. She has very distinct handwriting, and it was all over every card: LOVE, SANTA. I eventually figured out that Santa was a lie and it was devastating. However, that same year, the biggest present under the tree was for me (which was a nice trade-off). Once I started to open the present, I realized that this would be the gift that would keep on giving. My mother had stockpiled every stationery and craft supply under the sun and packed this box full. It took the entire day to empty it. I would make a craft with a few things from the box and then take a break. Then unpack some more and find something new to create with . . . Then the cycle repeated. One of the main items that I remember from this box was tape. Noticing all the different things I could do with it blew my mind—and still does. For this little travel item, I ask that you remember your little self, your practical self, and the self that fully and completely loves tape. **LEVEL** ◆◆

THE LINE-UP
- Duct tape (in at least 2 colors)
- Scissors
- Pillowcase
- Resealable freezer bags

THE BEGINNING
The last time you took an international flight, your face wash exploded and you had a bit of a mess on your hands in the hotel room. Not only did your skin pay the price of using a wash that your face did not love, but you regretted not using resealable freezer bags, because you had to toss your cosmetic bag. This time, pull out the resealable freezer bags—but why not jeuje them up? If nothing else, you will love making these fancy reusable bags. Head to the craft cupboard for duct tape and start your journey to taping nirvana.

THE MIDDLE
Lay down a pillowcase to use as a work surface, and start laying strips of tape, sticky side down, to create a large rectangular duct tape sheet a little bigger than your resealable bag. Make sure to overlap your tape pieces so they stick together. Peel the tape off the pillowcase to reveal a duct tape sheet. Once you've made two of these, place the plastic bag in between the tape sheets and stick them all together.

THE END To finish this off, trim around the edges to make the bag look clean and tidy. Now fold over a piece of duct tape the width of the bag and make a little fringe trim for the top! Your toiletries practically dance themselves inside this disco hologram bag to head away on vacation.

QUICK AND DIRTY
This little taped-up bag concept only takes a few minutes to complete and is truly an inexpensive, wipeable, and super-flashy, fun way to transport your cosmetics and toiletries without concern. Now you can take this concept and make many bags, large and small, the same way. This idea really is the tape gift that keeps on giving. Just like Christmas!

NOTE

Make sure to use this craft idea as a starting point for something that feels super cool and totally you! If you don't like an excessive use of trim, then try using just a simple ribbon, or maybe a string of sequins for something more blingy.

THE LINE-UP

- Hot glue gun
- Many, many trims
- Your simple black carry-on suitcase
- Scissors
- Pom poms (see page 87)

 2+ HRS

LUGGAGE & ALL THE TRIMMINGS

My mother is a flight attendant and has been since the good old days when flying was a privilege. She has always been picture-perfect in her appearance when flying, and while she is her own version of flamboyant, she also plays totally by-the-book. There is her practical heel for the airports and the flat shoe for onboard. She color-codes her uniform pocket square with the holidays and buys her own swizzle sticks and umbrellas to add to your in-flight cocktail. She is the reason that I became a flight attendant many years ago and also the reason that I own a black overhead compartment-sized roller-board suitcase! Now, I do not wear or own much black, but some things are "just practical," as she would say. But when I see something that is plain and totally mundane, I want to get my hands and hot glue gun all over it and make it my own! So, show your travel styles and give your fellow travelers something to talk about in the airport when you fully trim out your suitcase with a little hot glue, time, and extreme texture! Up, up, and away! LEVEL ◆◆

THE BEGINNING You are headed to Mexico for your sister's wedding and you're the maid of honor. Because of this role, you have to take your airport arrival seriously—which includes good visuals getting on and off the plane. Make sure that you have loads of hot glue sticks and raid your craft cupboard for just the right types of trims to blow everyone's minds. Plug in the glue gun and lay the trims out on a table. Put the suitcase on the table and get ready.

TIP

Sometimes the best-laid plans are not what you end up following in the end. Don't be too quick to run to the store for more supplies. The most magical things can happen when you let the project develop with what you have.

THE MIDDLE Run a strip of hot glue along the edges of the suitcase and then place the trim on top. Keep going until the suitcase looks like a party! Glue as much or as little trim as you like.

MORE

I have often found myself in a situation where I have gone a little too far on a craft and it feels like it has passed the point of no return. This means it is done. The more you add on, the cooler it will get, so when something has gone south just keep piling on the bedazzlements— this will save the day. Encrusted is better than busted.

THE END Once you're set with the amount of trim, add some pom poms to the roller board, and for some extra jeuje, wrap the suitcase handle in trim or yarn as well! Nobody else in the whole traveling world will have this suitcase, and it feels so good to know that you'll be showing up for this wedding with a one-of-a-kind bag, ready to help marry off your one-of-a-kind sister!

 # PASSPORT TO WOW

<1 HR

There is nothing that made me feel more accomplished in my twenties than all of the visas and stamps in my passport. I don't know why they meant so much to me, but they did. I looked at all the places I'd been like notches in my belt, but now I look at my passport as more of an external flash item. Very few people are really inspecting the inner details of my passport, so I cannot help but want the coolest passport holder to show my pro-traveler vibes. All it takes is a little embroidery thread and some glitter paper to turn a few frowns upside down in those long airport line-ups. **LEVEL** ◆◆

THE BEGINNING Off to Italy you go, and you want to have a little flash for not a lot of cash. If you don't have any glitter paper on-hand, get yourself to the craft store and pick some up. Grab your embroidery thread and an extra-thick and easy-to-thread needle.

THE LINE-UP
- Glitter paper
- Embroidery thread
- Large needle
- Scissors
- Paper tape
- A pencil
- Your passport!

NOTE
You can add patterns, shapes, or rhinestones onto this passport holder instead of preppy initials. The more bling, the better.

THE MIDDLE Take your passport, fold the glitter paper around it, and test-fit the paper so you know where to cut the paper and where to sew in your initials. Leave yourself a little extra room on each side so you know where to tape the paper to secure it to your passport when you're done. Now take your favorite colors of embroidery thread and map out a design or your initials on the back of the glitter paper with a pencil so you can follow your plan. Thread the needle and stitch over your pencil marks to turn your plan into a reality! If you like, you can use different colors of thread for the different letters.

THE END Once you've stitched your initials onto the passport holder, tape down the two flaps of the glitter paper that fold inside of the passport. Use some kind of paper tape so it doesn't interfere with the passport. If you want to take this project up a notch next time, buy some fabric and pull out your sewing machine. You'll be able to make a more permanent one just like it! *Bon voyage!*

FYI

Most of my crafting happens late at night. For some reason, this is the time that I feel the most creative and inspired. This also means that sometimes I make a few mistakes, because I stay up too late on a roll and then get sloppy. This is not a good late-night craft.

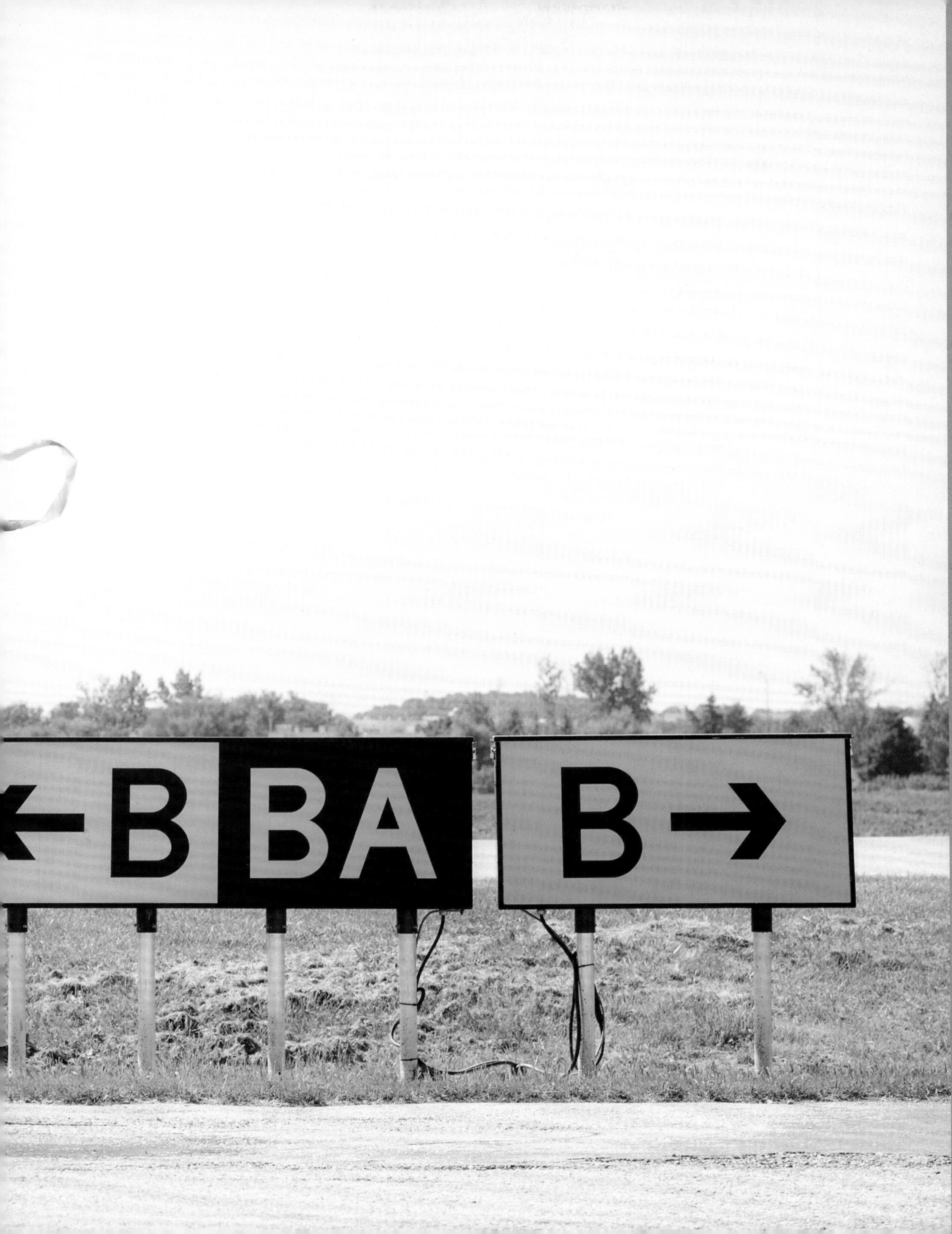
B
BA
B

PLACES I WANT TO GO AND THINGS I WANT TO MAKE ARE:

HANGIN' WITH THE
KIDS

This entire chapter is dedicated to the little people in our lives, and to the little person inside each of us who jumps out every once in a while to tell us to have more fun! In my late twenties, I was stuck in my career in fashion and cosmetics and somehow landed on the doorstep of an art studio for children. Being an artist all my life with no formal training, this scared the crap out of me—how could I teach art? Plus, I'd never hung around children before. The owner of the studio let me have a trial date, teaching children aged two to eight. And as soon as I entered the doors of this enchanted place I was hooked. I instantly understood on a deep level what it was like to be small, learning, and looking for amusement through colors, textures, and experiences. The year I spent teaching there ultimately inspired me to open up my own art studio for kids of all ages, called Glitter Pie. I taught everyone from age two straight to adults. Giving them the tools to try their own ways of approaching materials and creativity fed my soul and made me think even more deeply about everyday objects and how those could become art. That's the thing about kids; they teach you that everything can be something else.

At Glitter Pie, I made sure to teach in a way where the end result was less important than the process. I realized the importance of being true to myself and marveled at how children do it so effortlessly. I spend my life now out in the world in many ways, but when I need to get back to my center, I remember those humbling and groundbreaking moments on my studio floor, covered in paint, watching children discover textures and colors.

In this chapter, my biggest dream is for you to remember what it's like to be your littlest self. What stoked your fire when you were wee? What did it feel like to explore? More than anything, I hope you remember to forget what you think you know and instead look at life through new eyes. Consider that everything and anything is a moving, magical, available, and accessible piece of material, ready for you to make art and fun happen at every turn.

Now, let's go play.

DONUT HOLE NECKLACE

The first time I received a loot bag that had a candy necklace in it at a birthday party, my life changed forever. This singular concept captured two of my favorite things at once: candy and jewelry. Genius. I never forgot how pretty I felt wearing it, but that extra tummy butterfly was for when I reached down, stretched that elastic string, and took a bite out of it. Now I always think about how I can make something pretty and edible all at once, but my taste buds have altered a bit. I like candy a little less and baked goods a little more. Donuts are the super treat that I rely on when I need a real pick-me-up. One day I was eating a donut hole (a ball made out of donut dough and glaze) and realized that stringing some together would make one killer necklace. This is an amazing party activity, so let's jump off the invisible bridge together and find ourselves on candy-sprinkled sidewalks in our own private Candy Land, filled with edible-jewelry shops aplenty. LEVEL ◆◆◇

CONCEPT

Making wearables out of candy is something that I cannot get enough of. There is something about the juxtaposition that sweetens my creative heart. I urge you to make wearable art with candy and share it with your friends!

THE BEGINNING Raid your craft cupboard and your kitchen for all of the necessary supplies, then head to your local bakery. In the making of this craft, some donut holes will fall apart, so buy more than you think you'll need to ensure that you have enough to craft with, enough to destroy, and enough to eat while you work! This is very important!

THE MIDDLE Once you're home, cut a length of string suitable for a long necklace. Then grab a bamboo skewer and tape a piece of string to the end. Poke a hole in a donut hole and pull the skewer all the way through to thread the string through it. Once you have six to eight of these donut holes threaded on the string, tie it up, grab your plastic knife, and start to layer the white icing on the holes one at a time. Now dust or dunk colored sprinkles onto the white icing to make the donuts look a little bit more like beads, and adorn your neck with your necklace. This might be the most delicious-looking thing you have ever seen!

NOTE

For a neater approach, you can roll your iced donut holes inside little containers filled with sprinkles before you poke a hole in them and string them. I usually take the messy way. It's your choice. There are no rules here.

THE END Your counter is full of colored sprinkles and you are eating donut holes that are strung around your neck. You never thought that this level of awesome was possible, but today is your day. Happy donut day!

CANDY HEART STUDS

Ever since I was little, Valentine's Day has meant as much to me as my birthday, and my family treats it as such. Valentine's Day is my national holiday for all of the reasons that you can imagine. Everyone is celebrating love, writing sweet notes, and sending flowers. Heart-shaped boxes of chocolate run free and, if only for a day, the world looks like I imagine it should: pink, glittering, full of love, and filled with chocolate. Just typing these words makes me feel like jumping up and down in excitement. For this next craft, I continue to express my childlike love for edible jewelry. These edible candy heart stud earrings are sure to have everyone whispering sweet nothings into your ear. **LEVEL** ◆◆◆

THE BEGINNING Everyone passes out Valentine cards on Valentine's Day—but you are not everyone. You want to pass out edible candy heart studs to share with your friends, and this idea will be the star of the show! Head to a local jewelry store or craft store for earring supplies, and then get back to your place to start working for the big day!

THE LINE-UP

- Earring backs and posts
- Hot glue gun
- Piece of loose foam or bubble wrap
- Candy hearts
- Small pieces of cardstock

NOTE

I realize that not everyone has pierced ears, so while you're at the jewelry store getting the posts to make the earrings, you could pick up the clip-on earring backings too, so that your friends without pierced ears can also enjoy the sentiment!

THE MIDDLE Once your glue gun is hot and your home smells of sweet candy heart love, you can really get going. Organize matches by color, if you like, so that they look like real matching earrings. Grab the loose piece of foam or bubble wrap and stick the posts in it. Then, with a dab of glue, glue the candy hearts to the posts. If you're doing this craft with kids, be extra careful around the hot glue. Repeat until you have a pair of earrings for everyone you love, and let the glue dry.

THE END Gather pieces of cardstock and write love notes on them. Then poke holes in the cards and tack on your earrings. This idea is a treat for your friends, but better yet, it will encourage some sweet canoodling! HAPPY VALENTINE'S DAY!

BEWARE

If the kids shake these paper bags too hard, the egg might come out the bottom. If you know you have some aggressive shakers in the house, try using a resealable plastic bag for this craft instead.

SHAKE & BAKE EGGS

1+ HR

One of the treasured Pratt family home videos is of my two sisters and me dyeing Easter eggs when we were little. My mom looks so young and is buzzing around the kitchen getting a meal ready. My dad is chilling out, watching us, and letting all the antics go down. My younger sister, Chel, doesn't make a peep—she's engrossed in the process. My older sister, Jen, is livid with me because I was dipping my egg in all of the colored dyes at once. "Mommy! Tiffy is dipping the colors in the colors in the colors!!!" This family moment pretty much sums me up. I have always been dipping the colors in the colors in the colors, and this shake & bake craft is much the same. PS: I love eggs.   **LEVEL**

THE BEGINNING You're packing up your kids' lunches for the next day and you find the troops need a little entertainment as the day is winding down. There's no better way to dazzle up lunchtime than a shake & bake craft technique. Not every child likes hard-boiled eggs in their lunch, but if that egg is wrapped in aluminum foil and encrusted in confetti and glitter . . . At least they'll stop razzing you for writing love notes on their napkins (my mom did that!). Hard-boil your eggs and rip off strips of aluminum foil that are wide enough to wrap the egg completely.

THE MIDDLE Give the aluminum foil to the kids and let them wrap up all the eggs. In the meantime, fill up some paper bags with confetti, glitter, sequins, and candy sprinkles. You can use anything colorful and lightweight. Once you're ready, give each of the kids some white glue and a glue brush to paint the glue all over a foil-covered egg. Once it's completely covered in glue, hand them a paper bag that you just filled with the crafty contents. Then you tell them to lightly SHAKE IT UP!

THE END Once the kids have shaken the egg, they'll have baked it into a glittering colored sensation! Set the eggs in an egg carton in the fridge overnight to dry. This is a win-win craft: The kids are dazzled and want to make more, and you are thrilled because you now know how you can get them to eat eggs at school and glitter up their lunch hour!

THINK BIG

I like to to think of two-in-one ideas for the little ones. If you can give kids a project to bedazzle their lunch boxes, or really anything that they come in contact with more than once, they'll have a deeper connection to it and be proud of it, too!

PAPER POUCH

When I was little, my blanket, Bunnykins, and my mini Garfield backpack were among my most treasured items. I was obsessed with all these things, but the backpack was in a league of its own. I would strap that thing to my back as soon as I woke up, and I would hang it on the side of my bed at night just before going to sleep. This backpack had all of my loot inside it (if you know anything about little ones, you'll know that they love their treasures): mini Mary Kay lipstick samples, rocks or stones, candy (if I could get it), pens, pieces of paper, or anything else that would fit. Really, nothing has changed. I still have all of those things in my purse, only the size of my bag has increased . . . If you also love bags to store your treasures, here is a craft for you to do with or without a little one, because everyone should know how to make a paper purse! LEVEL ◆◆◇

THE LINE-UP

- Clear tape
- Newspaper
- Colored or metallic tape
- A stapler
- Double-sided self-adhesive Velcro

NOTE

You don't have to use newspaper for this craft; colored paper works well and so does old wrapping paper. Use what you have!

THE BEGINNING You're chilling with your niece and nephew for the afternoon and you've hosted a massive treasure hunt throughout the house to keep them busy. You filled the place with all kinds of morsels that would set their hearts on fire: candy, toy cars, plastic bracelets, tiny gemstones, and more. Now that they have their collections of loot from the hunt, you realize that you need to create a place for this stuff to go! Pull out the newspaper and tell your peeps that you're going to make pouches out of newspaper. Lay down overlapping strips of clear packing tape so that you've created multiple sheets and lay them on the table sticky side up. Now lay the newspaper on top.

THE MIDDLE Fold the tape-covered newspaper in half and staple up the sides to make a pouch. Then show your peeps the colored tape and have them tape up the edges over the staples so it is safer and looks prettier. Once they've taped up the edges (and all over the pouch, for that matter), it's time to put the double-sided Velcro on so that these pouches can stay shut. Give each of them a pre-cut strip of Velcro and have them attach it to the opening wherever they like.

THE END Once these pouches have the closure sorted, they're ready for stuffing full of all of the treasures that were found. When your sister comes over to collect her kids from your place, it's like you organized some DIY loot bag concept and you are a hit! Hosting activities for kids is your thing now and you cannot wait to babysit again soon!

1+ HR

ART IN A BOX

When I closed my art studio many years ago, I knew that my work with children wasn't finished. I wanted kids to continue creating in an authentic way outside of my studio and have easy access to all the things that could inspire them. I began another venture called Glitter Pie Art Studio in a Box and it was all about capturing my favorite crafting things in one box so that parents didn't have to run around to a bunch of stores to collect all they would need to craft at home. Every box was created one-of-a-kind and was hand-packed (by me for the first 500) to ensure that it was filled with love and magic. This effort was made so that children could pull out this art box anytime and glue and glitter to their hearts' content. I urge you to make a kit to keep at the ready for the little people in your life. If you have the essentials all stocked, packed, and collected in one place, you'll be thrilled to see what can be done with what you've organized for your little person. The results will be magical and you will use this little art box as your most powerful artillery when the boredom blues come knocking. **LEVEL** ◆◆◇

THE LINE-UP

- White glue
- Glue brush
- Glitter
- Craft paper/newspaper (to use as a drop cloth)
- Assorted fabrics, sequins, scissors, colored feathers, faux flowers, trims and yarn, pretty papers, cardstock, and LOVE

THE BEGINNING You have little ones in your life and you need to be prepared. Your daughter could craft all night and she blows through basic craft kits like nobody's business! But she's also a kid on the go, and sometimes has need of a crafting to-go collection. The solution? Gather some of her favorite stuff from the craft cupboard—this way you can bring the art everywhere you go! It's great to start by asking her what she loves so you know what to collect and pack. You can make some suggestions, too, or bring her along on a trip to a craft store to pick out materials for her kit.

THE MIDDLE Once you've packed the kit, remember that a handy drop cloth is the way to ensure a fast and easy cleanup. So make sure to add in some newspapers or craft paper. Maybe even include a plastic bag so you have a place to collect all the cleanup mess.

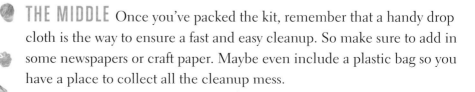

THE END This kit has saved your life over and over. Check on the contents a few times each week to keep it fresh and new. Also make sure your little one treats it with love and care, and that she tidies it as often as she can so she knows what she has and what she needs more of. It's important for her to take ownership of it, give you reports on its status, and even share the kit among many of her pals.

SET UP FOR ART

2+ HRS

One of the things that I thank my mom for was always giving my sisters and me a place to create and play. Between the cake decorating tools, sewing kits, paints, and more, there was a ton of random supplies and a big table that served us well growing up. As I got older, the activities moved to my bedroom walls and closet doors. Then they moved again, to the walls of my high school where I painted murals and stained-glass windows. Setting the stage for creating is the most important thing you can do for your young creators and yourself. Think of your creating place as the most sacred space that you can imagine for both you and your children. Set it up, leave it tidy, stock it up, and romance it with some new materials from time to time. When you set up for art, you set yourself up for love. **LEVEL** ◆◆◆

GOOD IDEAS

Children appreciate beautiful things and want to be a part of making them happen. Never underestimate the power of a child's sense of style, participation, and appreciation.

THE LINE-UP

- Comfortable and easy-to-clean chairs and working space
- Shelf space
- Jars
- Newspaper, craft paper, markers, pens, paper tape, crayons, paints, painting paper, canvas, paintbrushes, cloths, and glitter!

THE BEGINNING Your house needs a space for your little ones to hunker down and create because you would rather your children create than sit in front of the TV or play on their phones. You know that if you create a wonder-filled area for them to be, they will hover there instead of heading straight to the computer. You have a simple worktable and a little shelf, so set up this furniture in the center of your living space and get rolling on making it magic!

CLEANLINESS IS NEXT TO GODLINESS

A creative space is a tidy place. Not many people believe this philosophy, but I know after years of teaching that it is true. If everyone in your family makes an effort to keep the space tidy, it will always be ready for spontaneous creation!

THE MIDDLE Collect all of the art supplies from around the house, then start gathering extra jars to organize the craft supplies. It's always more inspiring when materials are displayed beautifully. Allocate some newspaper and a few tea towels for quick and easy cleanup. Ask your little ones how they would like things organized and where things should go. Consult your children and get them involved in decisions. It empowers them, and when their thoughts are required they will develop great decision-making skills and ownership over their choices.

THE END The details are everything in any crafting project, so add a pretty shelf to the wall to organize the inspirations, art supplies, and treasures for your little ones to see. If you want to take it one step further, hang some fairy lights and garlands to set the scene for the big creative space reveal. Have your kids help you set up the space so you can all be excited about it. Doing things together is team-building and collaborative and will result in an amazing art empire!

CENTER STAGE

If you place a making space or table in a high-traffic area of your home, your children will gravitate there because they'll feel like they're in the middle of the action. As soon as you relegate this kind of spot to the basement, you'll find it unlikely that your kids will frequent this crafting heaven. Take the plunge and put it in the center of your space (at least for the time being), and you'll find that creating becomes king and screens will be for later.

ME & THE LITTLE PEOPLE IN MY LIFE WILL MAKE:

FINAL THOUGHTS

The people, places, and things in life that you do not see coming can be the ones that change you forever. I had the most life-altering experience working with children at a time in my life when I was unaware of how ready for a transformation I was. I was taken back to the beginning, and was able to revisit my life with that sense of childlike wonder all over again. Ending this book with a kids' chapter is a purposeful and powerful decision for me. If I had not had the time that I did creating with children, I would never have realized that the real joy comes from the process of making, not necessarily the result. Children taught me to see play and possibility in most anything.

This Can Be Beautiful is about returning to our true and little selves. It's about loving and accepting who we are, and making magic with the tools we have at hand. Children can make something out of nothing every time. They can turn a stick into a wand and wish on a petal. And, now, as your fairy godmother of glitter, I wish for you to take steps every day to return to a place inside of yourself and the place inside your home that is filled with treasures ready for you to celebrate and use. Embrace the life you always wanted while using what you already have. Wave your own magic wand, become your own fairy godmother, and little by little, develop that mantra for yourself. All you have to do is remember: *This Can Be Beautiful.*

ACKNOWLEDGMENTS

I knew the title of this book before I had even written it. Deep inside of me this book and its message already existed. And because of a village of believers, magicians, dreamers, and makers, this book is in your hands and a dream turned into reality. I am BIG on gratitude, and my daily practice is thanking as many people as I can think of for everything they do, big or small. I will stop myself from making these pages a sonnet of sappy and stick to my book angels only. Here we go:

To my Family: Peeps (Mom), Pratta (Jen) and Beans (Chel). I don't have enough pages in this book to tell each of you how much I love you. I don't have enough words to express my gratitude for your existence. I don't have enough colors on my palette to paint a master-piece that could do justice to the spectrum of inspiration, support and strength that each of you have colored into my world. Thank you.

Tara McMullen: you believed in this book before I had even written it. Thank you for forcing me to buy the websites to match my dreams. Thank you for capturing all the magic in this book, thank you for the time and love you poured into it. Nobody could have done it like you.

Adria Vasil: you had me at "Hello." Thank you for telling me I could write a book and for introducing me to Robert McCullough. Your beautiful friendship and "full power love" mean the world to me.

Judy Linden: I cried so hard the day I left your office when you said you would be the agent for this book. Your work, support, and belief in me and this message have meant more than I could ever say to you.

Robert McCullough: from the moment we met I knew I was in the presence of great-ness. I thank you for meeting me that fine day and giving me and my book proposal a chance. Thank you for every meeting we had in all the years that passed until you could not pass up on making this book.

Zoe Maslow: the book world gifted me the largest prize when I finally made it to you in this process. I could have never prepared for the high blessing of having the best editor and now the best of friends. *Beshert!*

Kelly Hill: you created a book that was an amplified version of my original idea, and I cannot thank you enough for supporting all my visions and making the visual dream of this book come to life in every way possible.

Cathy Paine: without your support in this book I am unsure how it could have made it into the hands of or in front of so many. Thank you from the bottom of my heart for every ounce of support.

Claire Gilbert: thank you for being in my corner and quietly and consistently supporting every little creation and crazy idea. You help me make my dreams come true every day. You're my angel from Down Under.

Becky DeOliveira: you are my friend and flower pimp. Having your genius touch throughout these pages is very meaningful to me. I love you, dude.

You: most of all, you. Thank you. Thank you for opening your heart and purchasing this book. I am grateful for the chance to have been in your life in some way. I LOVE YOU.

INDEX

A

acrylic paint. *See also* paint
    Canvas to Clutch! 58–59
    Cardboard Cards, 88–89
    Cereal Box Treasure, 84–85
Art in a Box, 152–53
art supplies, organizing, 154–55

B

Bag Tag Blitz, 126–27
bangles. *See* cuff, toilet paper roll
bath salts, 66–67
beads
    Napkin Ring Necklace, 112–13
beauty products, 65–79
bindis. *See also* gemstones;
  rhinestones
    Furniture Pad Studs, 18–19
bleached clothing, 48–49
body oil, 74–75
body scrub, 78–79
Bows, Pink Bubble,
  96–97
bracelets. *See* cuff, toilet paper roll
bubble wrap bows, 96–97

C

Candy Heart Studs, 144–45
cans. *See* soda cans
Canvas to Clutch! 58–59
Cardboard Cards, 88–89
cellophane
    Cracker Curiosity, 86–87
Cereal Box Treasure, 84–85

chalk
    Hair Powder for Days, 70–71
Clean Slate Salt Bath, 66–67
clothing. *See also* fashion
    bleached, 48–49
    cut, 60–61
Clutch, Canvas, 58–59
Clutch, Pillowcase, 16–17
Coffee Filter Flourish, 124–25
Color-In, Wallpaper, 36–37
confetti
    Bag Tag Blitz, 126–27
    Light Switch Facelift, 12–13
    Setting the Table, 114–15
    Shake & Bake Eggs, 148–49
Cosmetic Bag Tape-Up, 130–31
costume jewelry. *See also individual*
  jewelry types
    House Numerology, 34–35
    Off the Cuff, 56–57
Cracker Curiosity, 86–87
cuff, toilet paper roll, 56–57
Curtain, Scrap Fabric, 38–39
Curtain, String, 24–25
cut clothing, 60–61

D

Donut Hole Necklace, 142–43
duct tape
    Cosmetic Bag Tape-Up, 130–31
dye. *See* fabric dye; food coloring;
  tie-dyed sheets

E

earrings, candy heart, 144–45
earrings, furniture pad, 18–19
eggs, decorated, 148–49

embroidery thread
    Coffee Filter Flourish, 124–25
    Passport to Wow, 134–35
essential oils. *See* oils, essential

F

fabric dye
    bleached clothing, 48–49
    tie-dyed sheets, 30–31
fabric scraps
    Art in a Box, 152–53
    Light Switch Facelift, 12–13
    Loot Jars, 108–9
    Paper Bag Priestess, 94–95
    Scrap Fabric Curtain, 38–39
    Super Power Scrub, 78–79
fashion, 47–61
feathers
    Art in a Box, 152–53
    Setting the Table, 114–15
flowers, faux
    Art in a Box, 152–53
    Setting the Table, 114–15
food coloring
    with glue as alternative to Mod
      Podge, 13
    TP Streamers, 110–11
Furniture Pad Studs, 18–19
Furniture Paint-Up, Big, 14–15

G

Garland Land, 104–5
Garment Bag Swag, 122–23
gemstones. *See also* costume
  jewelry; rhinestones
    Furniture Pad Studs, 18–19
    House Numerology, 34–35
    Napkin Ring Necklace, 112–13

gift bags, 94–95
gift boxes, 84–85
gift cards, 84, 88–89
gifts, 83–97
glitter
    Art in a Box, 152–53
    Bag Tag Blitz, 126–27
    Furniture Pad Studs, 18–19
    Glitter Ho-Siery, 52–53
    House Numerology, 34–35
    Light Switch Facelift, 12–13
    Message in a Glass, 102–3
    Nail Polish Mix-Up, 68–69
    Pink Bubble Bows, 96–97
    Shake & Bake Eggs, 148–49
    Super Power Scrub, 78–79
glitter glue
    Loot Jars, 108–9
glitter paper
    Passport to Wow, 134–35
greenery
    Setting the Table, 114–15

H

Hair Powder for Days,
    70–71
hair rollers, soda can, 76–77
home décor, 29–43
Ho-Siery, Glitter, 52–53
hostess gifts, 92–93
House Numerology,
    34–35

I

icing rose rings, 50–51
invitations, party, 102–3

J

jewelry. *See* costume jewelry;
    individual jewelry types

K

kids' projects, 141–155

L

lace. *See also* trims
    Paper Bag Priestess, 94–95
Light Switch Facelift, 12–13
Loot Jars, 108–9
Luggage & All the Trimmings,
    132–33
luggage, rosettes for, 124–25
luggage tags, 126–27

M

Message in a Glass, 102–3
Mirror Caddy, 40–41
Mod Podge
    alternative for, 13
    Light Switch Facelift, 12–13

N

nail polish
    Furniture Pad Studs, 18–19
    Nail Polish Mix-Up, 68–69
Napkin Ring Necklace, 112–13
Necklace, Donut Hole, 142–43
Necklace, Napkin Ring, 112–13
newspaper pouch, 150–51

O

Off the Cuff, 56–57
oils, essential
    Clean Slate Salt Bath, 66–67
    Skin Potion #9, 74–75
organizing art supplies, 154–55

P

paint. *See also* acrylic paint; spray
    paint; watercolor paint
    Big Furniture Paint-Up, 14–15
    Mirror Caddy, 40–41
pantyhose, glitter, 52–53
Paper Bag Priestess, 94–95
Paper Pouch, 150–51
paper towel rolls
    Cracker Curiosity, 86–87
party supplies and décor, 101–16
Passport to Wow, 134–35
pegboard mirror caddy, 40–41
Pillowcase Clutch, 16–17
pillowcases, tie-dyed, 30–31
Pink Bubble Bows, 96–97
pom poms
    Cracker Curiosity, 86–87
    Loot Jars, 108–9
    Luggage & All the Trimmings,
    132–33
    Message in a Glass, 102–3
pom poms, DIY, 87
Punch Bowl Spray-Out, 22–23
purses
    canvas, 58–59
    paper, 150–51
    pillowcase, 16–17

R

rhinestones. *See also* gemstones
    House Numerology, 34–35
    Off the Cuff, 56–57
    Passport to Wow, 134–35
ribbon. *See also* trims
    Cereal Box Treasure, 84–85
    Cracker Curiosity, 86–87
    House Numerology, 34–35
    Luggage & All the Trimmings,
      132–33
    Mirror Caddy, 40–41
    Napkin Ring Necklace, 112–13
    Off the Cuff, 56–57
    Paper Bag Priestess, 94–95
    Super Power Scrub, 78–79
Rings, Rose-Arty, 50–51
Rose-Arty Rings, 50–51
rose petals
    Clean Slate Salt Bath, 66–67
rosettes, coffee filter, 124–25
Rug Spray-Out, 42–43

S

Salt Bath, Clean Slate, 66–67
Scrap Fabric Curtain, 38–39
sequins
    Art in a Box, 152–53
    Garment Bag Swag, 122–23
    Luggage & All the Trimmings,
      132–33
    Shake & Bake Eggs, 148–49
Setting the Table, 114–15
Shake & Bake Eggs, 148–49
sheets, tie-dyed, 30–31

Skin Potion #9, 74–75
soda cans
    Mirror Caddy, 40–41
    Soda Can Roller Delight, 76–77
spray paint. *See also* paint
    Mirror Caddy, 40–41
    Punch Bowl Spray-Out, 22–23
    Rug Spray-Out, 42–43
Streamers, TP, 110–11
streamers as table decorations,
    114–15
String Curtain, 24–25
Super Power Scrub, 78–79

T

table-setting ideas, for parties,
    114–15
tie-dyed sheets, 30–31
tips and tools, 6–9
tissue paper
    Cracker Curiosity, 86–87
    Light Switch Facelift, 12–13
    Setting the Table, 114–15
toilet paper rolls
    Cracker Curiosity, 86–87
    Off the Cuff, 56–57
    TP Streamers, 110–11
tools and tips, 6–9
TP Streamers, 110–11
travel gear, 121–135
trims. *See also* ribbon
    Art in a Box, 152–53
    Luggage & All the Trimmings,
      132–33
    Paper Bag Priestess, 94–95

W

wallpaper
    Light Switch Facelift, 12–13
    Wallpaper Color-In, 36–37
washi tape
    Garment Bag Swag, 122–23
watercolor paint. *See also* paint
    Coffee Filter Flourish, 124–25
wire
    Pink Bubble Bows,
      96–97
wrapping paper
    Cracker Curiosity, 86–87
    Paper Pouch, 150–51

Y

yarn
    Art in a Box, 152–53
    Cereal Box Treasure, 84–85
    Loot Jars, 108–9
    pom poms, DIY, 87